THE STORYTELLING CHURCH

The Storytelling Church

ADVENTURES IN RECLAIMING THE ROLE OF STORY IN WORSHIP

Jeff Barker

WEBBER INSTITUTE BOOKS

2011

Webber Institute Books
121 Holly Trail Road, NW
Cleveland, Tennessee 37311

The Storytelling Church:
Adventures in Reclaiming the Role of Story in Worship

ISBN 978-1-936912-29-2

This book constitutes the inaugual volume of the Webber Institute Books Series.

To order additional copies of this book, contact:

Parson's Porch Books
1-423-475-7308
www.parsonsporchbooks.com

Webber Institute Books
is an imprint of
Parson's Porch Books

for Jon Opgenorth,
much loved pastor and friend
who knows the stories behind
so many of the stories recounted here

Contents

WEBBER INSTITUTE BOOKS

Webber Institute Books serves as the publishing arm of the Robert E. Webber Institute for Worship Studies (IWS), which was founded by the late Robert E. Webber for the purpose of forming servant leaders in worship renewal with the perspective that "the way to the future necessarily runs through the past." IWS is the only school in North America dedicated solely to graduate education in the biblical foundations, historical development, theological reflection, and cultural analysis of worship. Its vision emphasizes that its graduates will "participate intentionally in the story of the Triune God" in order to "bring renewal in the local and global church by shaping life and ministry according to the fullness of that story." In scope it is "evangelical in nature and ecumenical in outlook, embracing and serving the whole church in its many expressions and variations." Those interested in obtaining further information concerning the Institute should consult its website at www.iws.edu.

Webber Institute Books are published by agreement with Parson's Porch Books (www.parsonsporchbooks.com) in order to provide a means for disseminating to the general public varying and differing views concerning the many aspects of worship and Christian life. The ideas expressed in these published materials wholly remain the views of the authors themselves and are not necessarily those of either IWS or the publisher.

It is the prayerful concern of both IWS and the publisher that the information contained in these works will stimulate further reflection and discussion. The results of such exchange of ideas hopefully will enhance worship renewal within the various segments of the Christian church. Moreover, in keeping with the hopes and dreams of Bob Webber may all that is done through this publishing enterprise enable Christians to reject the narcissistic patterns prevalent in contemporary society and give the glory to God who sent Jesus, the Christ, to provide for human transformation and in concert provided humans with the divine triune presence through the Holy Spirit.

Gerald L. Borchert
General Editor

James R. Hart
President of IWS

Acknowledgments

The following groups have been so helpful: the members of Trinity Reformed Church in Orange City, Iowa, including the TRC worship teams, the worship support teams and the worship planning teams; the members over several school years and summers of the Northwestern College Drama Ministries Ensemble (and those who hosted their performances); the staff at the Calvin Institute of Christian Worship and the members of the summer seminar on teaching worship sponsored by CICW; the students in my Drama and Worship classes for 2005 and 2007, and the students in Worship class at Western Theological Seminary in 2002; my wonderful colleagues in the Northwestern College theatre and speech department, including several treasured student assistants; and the attendees at the worship and writing workshops held at the DeWitt Theatre Arts Center. When I have included writings generated at these workshops, I have done so with each author's permission.

I want especially to mention the members of our teaching church project's final semester: Lois Estell, Shirley Folkerts, Meg Hodgin, Andy Keller, Kristen Olson-Jones, Tessa Rosier, and Kristi Woodyard.

There are so many individuals who have shaped and supported me in this journey. I would like especially to thank the following, and they each know the role they have played: Bruce and Adel Aiken, Jonathan Allsup, Michael Andres, Arthur and Bette Barker, Paul and Mary Ann Blezien, Doris Bohm, Tom Boogaart, Tim Brown, Doug Carlson, Marion Clark, Stu and

Mary Clark, Joe and Caryl Culumber, Solomon Davis, Sherri DeBoom, Don and Cindy DeGlopper, Don and Audrey Den Hartog, Laird and Sally Edman, Marsha Floding, Deb Freeburg, Tamara Fynaardt, Bev Heemstra, Trygve Johnson, Laurie Kurtz, Jim Mead, Jon Nelson, Dennis Rockhill, Greg Scheer, Arlene Schuiteman, Lin Sexton, Lila Simmelink, Lynn and Joonna Trapp, Kristin Trease, Eleanor Vandevort, Kelly Van Marel, Harlan Van Oort, Jeanette Van Voorst, and John Witvliet. Many others who played important roles can be found mentioned within the pages of this book.

Keith Anderson, Susan Rees, and Dave Nonnemacher have each been leaders of the Vocare project at Northwestern over the past few years, and I am deeply grateful for their support and encouragement.

Scriptures cited are from the New International Version unless otherwise indicated.

Some of the stories in this book were seen in earlier versions (and even under alternate titles) in other publications, including *The Church Herald* (One Pastor's Wife's Saturday), *Perspectives* (The Other Driver), *Catapult Magazine* (Danyale's Wedding), and *Christianity and Theatre* (Danyale's Wedding; No Regard for the Deeds of the Lord). Some of the chapters were released for a time on my blog at http://storyandworship.wordpress.com. And an earlier version of the entire book was released under the title *Quiet Demons and Screaming Peter Pan*.

My students and colleagues at the Robert E. Webber Institute for Worship Studies have been encouraging and helpful throughout the latter stages of the development of this book.

Jerry Borchert was a generous, wise, expert, creative, and gracious editor for this project. He is also a prince of a person, and I am deeply indebted to him.

John Eric Killinger is the exceptionally professional, helpful, and patient editor for Parson's Porch Books who saw this inaugural volume of Webber Institute Books through to completion.

Finally, I am so grateful for my family: Joseph and Hannah each read chunks of this book without prompting from their dad, Daniel keeps me honest, and my beloved Karen's heartbeat, wit and wisdom resound throughout these pages.

INTRODUCTION

The Dream of Being Known in Church

Now I know in part; then I shall know fully, even as I am fully known.

— 1 Corinthians 13:12b

When I was in graduate school, I traveled to northern Wisconsin and met the great American theatre director Paul Sills. Sills was the founding director of Chicago's improvisational theatre, The Second City. Even though Sills is unknown outside the profession, he has directed and taught so many who have become luminaries. He also developed the theatrical form known as "story theatre."

I was writing my thesis about Paul's career. I had come to revere him so much I was terrified to meet him. In fact, a few people I interviewed told me Paul would never talk to me, or if he did, he might respond petulantly.

I pulled my car up next to the barn where for years Paul had led classes on improvisational acting. I got out, looked toward the house and there he was, the icon, standing in the doorway. I stumbled up to him and stood there, speechless.

I figured he would at least throw a chair at me.

He reached out a gracious hand and said, "I'm Paul." Then he pulled me up the steps into his kitchen where he said, "I'll make you a sandwich." He saved my life. We ultimately had a lovely conversation, sans petulance. At one point, he said, "I'm applying for a teaching job. Give me your response to the way I've done my résumé. I haven't done one of these before." The document he placed in front of me was in longhand. He was the cliché artistic personality—an alien in a market-driven culture.

Paul's discomfiture became especially palpable to me a year later when I finished my first year of teaching at Geneva College, a small Christian liberal arts college in Pennsylvania. Karen and I traveled back to Chicago to visit family and see some plays. I discovered Paul Sills had returned to the Windy City, and a play of his was running in the little theatre off the alley behind The Second City mainstage. Here was my chance to see the great man's work. We made reservations. When we arrived at the box office, there, selling the tickets, was Paul himself. I reintroduced myself. He asked me what I was doing now. I told him I had just finished my first year of teaching college theatre. I felt ashamed in the face of his significance, but when I looked at him, he had a shy grin on his face. He said, "I wish I had a job like that."

Paul's work and words have continued to influence my life. It was at the farm that he said, almost offhandedly, "Stories contain the truth and wisdom of the ages." That is a truth I almost missed. I grew up in a church that taught the Bible contained the truth and wisdom of the ages. As a child, I understood this to mean truth was found in the form of argument, proof-text and bumper stickers. It took a liberal arts education to convince me all truth was God's truth, wherever it may be found. It was years later, years after I met Paul Sills, when I finally came to understand that all beauty is God's beauty, and truth might appear in artistic form. This reality was right in front of my face all along—in the stories of the Hebrew Bible and the parables of Jesus.

The worshiping tradition of my childhood focused on reverencing Jesus through song, offering, prayer and persuasion. Story was primarily relegated to children's Sunday School. Story, to my recall, did not have a prominent place in my home church's most formative arena—its public worship.

You will see as you read this book that I have not changed my mind about Jesus, but I have changed my mind about story.

This book is for those who wish to think about the place of story in worship. It is a book about worship and story, and it is also a book of stories. (In other words, I am trying to put my money where my mouth is. I aim to do what I say.)

You may read the chapters in any order. Each will tell its own tale. And, as the wonderful contemporary memoirist Dennis Covington says, our lives themselves are stories. The stories of this book will add up—they will tell the larger story of my life's worship journey thus far.

Sometimes I will focus on worship itself, but usually I will focus on the edge where worship touches story and storytelling. I am speaking of story in at least the following specific ways: Bible story, history, parable, personal story, faith story, story as an art form, and finally, story as worship structure, meaning the story form of the whole worship service.

I am attempting to encourage those who worship and those who lead other worshipers to ask this simple question: What should we do about story?

To tone down the potential for arrogance and polarization in this journey we are about to take, I would like to invite you sideways to a book about writing. In *Writing Down the Bones*, Natalie Goldberg says,

Learning to write is not a linear process. There is no log-
ical A-to-B-to-C way to become a good writer. One neat
truth about writing cannot answer it all (1986:4).

It seems to me that what Goldberg says here about writing is also true of worship. This worshipful path is not straight. There is no logical way to become a good worshiper. Worship is as messy as living. Worship is, as A. W. Tozer says, the reason we are alive—our purpose on this earth—but there is no one neat and true answer to how to do worship or how to lead others in doing worship.

In her book on writing, Goldberg explains that she is attempting to help writers access "the essential, awake speech of their minds." The worship leader in me is reminded of the phrase "full, conscious, and active participation," which is the goal for worshipers described in Vatican II's *Sacrosanctum Concilium* (1963).

Goldberg's suggestion for authentic writing is to "Write down the bones." A writer who is writing down the bones is putting the inner life down on the page. The inside is turned outward, and what is written reveals the basic truth of the person.

My suggestion for authentic worship is to "worship out the bones"—to bring the inner life out in our worship, all the way to the "spirit and truth" of which Jesus spoke. You may think I am saying that true worship is from the very bones, as in "worship out [of] the bones." Such would be really passionate worship. There is nothing wrong with passion in worship, but I am trying for a more mystical image. I am picturing a vulnerable worship, in which the worshiper is willing to acknowledge reality as God knows it to be. The honest to goodness truth comes out in this kind of worship in which the inner, God-seen life is turned outward. The skeletons come out of the closet.

It is a gruesome image, but think of Ezekiel's valley of dry bones being imbued with spirit, and you will be able to let your mind wander into such territory. Think of Psalm 103, "He knows our frame; he remembers that we are dust."

I am striving toward an image which no longer expects worship to be all dressed up in "Sunday-go-to-meeting clothes." This worship is as hospitable and honest as an Alcoholics Anonymous meeting.

How does it work? We tell our stories. "Hi my name is Jeff, and I'm a sinner. Here's what happened. . . ."

Goldberg says she wants to write down the bones because, "I want someone to know me. We walk through so many myths of each other and ourselves; we are so thankful when someone sees us for who we are and accepts us" (1986:21).

I want someone to know me. I want God to know me. I want you to know me. I want to worship out the bones.

"Bones-out" worship is essential.

> Awake.
> Full.
> Conscious.
> Active.
> Participatory.
> True.

I do not know how to get there without telling our stories. But this book is no prescription. There is no one way to write. There is no one way to love. There is no one way to worship. Am I being a relativist? I hope not. I do believe we can say there are ways you cannot worship God. You cannot worship God with human sacrifice. You cannot worship God with an act of injustice. You cannot worship God by worshiping God's creation. The list goes on. True worship is true love of God, and therefore, has as many variations as there are lovers.

I would like to hear your love story.

What do the bones look like in your own worship? Your answer might include:

> affection for God,
> sadness for your sins,
> gratefulness for God at work,
> helplessness without God,
> grief for where God is not yet,
> submission to God's assignments,
> giddy celebration over God.

All of these bones (and more) make up the skeletal structure of our relationship with God. Can we reveal each of these "bones" every time we worship? No. Perhaps, however, we can strive for such revelations over a life of worship.

If we are not willing to worship out the bones, may we still call it worship?

One of the most reasonable ways to accomplish "bones-out" worship is through storytelling. Can we tell each other some stories? Can at least one song move over each Sunday to make room?

Many of us in the church have been away from hearing and telling stories so long that we are confused about getting started. Perhaps believing it should be difficult, we confess we do not have the slightest idea how to start.

In my experience, getting started is actually pretty simple. You start by saying, "I'd love to hear what your life has been like." With trust and sensitivity as our protectors, these personal stories can soon find their way into the fabric of our public life together.

Until I was five, my parents took us eight kids to a Baptist church. There was an article in the paper which included a picture of the Barker family taking up an entire pew. But that church apparently was not separatist enough, so my parents helped start a non-denominational, fundamentalist Bible church, which nurtured and nagged me until college. Somewhere in there, I learned to study the Bible, I made some private and public professions of faith and I was baptized. I went away to a Free Methodist college. During my first year at college, I was a youth leader at a Presbyterian church. About this time, my sister was telling me of her experiences in the charismatic Jesus movement of southern California. Then my college art professor took us into a Catholic cathedral in St. Louis where I saw centuries-old mosaics and walked the stations of the cross for the first time. It devastated me. I did not have a box for Christ's church anymore.

It was on a Sunday night during those college years when I heard Donald Bastian preach a sermon about what heaven may be like. I had not yet become rooted in Reformed theology, and Dr. Bastian had not yet become a Bishop of the Free Methodist Church. I was just a college student afraid of losing his faith, and Reverend Bastian was just a pastor of the college church. On the Sunday night in question, he said that he believes when we are in heaven, we will know everyone as we are known. In other words, our personalities will be hanging out for everyone to see. Pastor Bastian said he did not know how it would happen, but he believed it would be true. There would no longer be the need for secrets, and finally, we could be known. I was terrified of the idea, but I also knew that he was describing what I wanted.

I have come to believe that Dr. Bastian was right, and, as with the journey of sanctification, we should not wait for heaven. We should start now.

CHALLENGES

A Famine of the Spirit

Go home to your friends, and tell them how much the Lord
has done for you, and what mercy he has shown you.
— Mark 5:19b, NRSV

When I was a freshman in college, I went on a mission trip to Haiti. It was my first time out of the country, and I fell in love with the place and the people. It was very difficult to come home. As I started my sophomore year of college, I did not know how to handle the lavish wealth of my own country. I gave away my valuables (my clothes and my tennis racket). I wore bib overalls most of that year.

That year I wrote my first play as an attempt to sort it out. It was a terrible play, and I will never let you see it. But I will tell you the names of the characters: Coin Man, Starving Man, Bread Man, Coat Man, and Trash Man. The action of the play involved a man with a coin attempting to buy some bread for a starving man, but getting talked into buying a coat for himself instead. In the end, Starving Man dies and Trash Man hauls the corpse away. On the back of the coat, I sewed an image of a cross, like a stained glass window. I titled the play *Worship*.

Do you think it was blatant enough?

I was trying to grapple with what it means to be a worshiper in a world of magnificent church buildings where people who do not have bread to eat. This problem was significant for someone who felt called to be an artist and spend his life creating beauty.

My solution did not come quickly or easily, and in some sense the tension between pragmatics and aesthetics is always with us whether we are in the arts or automobile repair. I have had a variety of helpers in my struggle. One story that has been especially valuable to me is what happened to Morgan Jenness. Morgan is a dramaturge and a literary agent. I discovered her story hidden in an interview in a book entitled *Dramaturgy in American Theater*. (Dramaturgy, for the uninitiated, is the literary and historical analysis of plays.) I passed the story along to my colleague and wife, Karen, who loves to tell it to our theatre students. And I thought you might like to hear it as well. So I wrote to Morgan and asked if I could share it with you. Here it is, in her own words:

> *When I was in my early twenties, I was still working part-time doing computer entry and working at the Public [Theater] a couple days a week. I had been trying to perform and was wondering what my life in the theatre was really about. I decided it was all nonsense and that I really wanted to do something more meaningful with my life. So, I got it into my head I was going to join Mother Teresa's Sisters of Mercy in Calcutta, and that I was going to pick up dying people off the streets, and own nothing but a sari and a bucket, and give my life to service. I was right in the middle of trying to figure out how I was going to get to India when it turned out that Mother Teresa was making a trip to New York. Then I was beside myself trying to figure out how to meet her. I called up her place in the Bronx, but they didn't know her exact itinerary. I checked the papers and called up places she had visited, but nobody knew where she was going next. One of the people at my computer job sug-*

gested I call the Indian Consulate. I thought, if her convent doesn't know, why would the Indian Consulate? But I called, and the person who answered the phone said, "Yes, as a matter of fact, she's going to be at the Consulate in about an hour to address the staff here." Bingo. I believe it was late spring . . . a beautiful day. I remember saying to everyone around me, "That's it. I'm going. I'm going to meet Mother Teresa and I probably won't be back. Bye!" I dashed there—it was off Fifth Avenue in the sixties or seventies. A guard was standing outside, and I asked him if Mother Teresa had come yet. He said she hadn't. About three minutes later two cars pulled up. She got out of the first one, with these tall men, and a whole flock of nuns got out of the second one. They came walking up the street toward me. I was now practically hearing choirs of angels in my head. She was tiny and had these eyes like burning coals. She looked at me and motioned for me to follow them in. I followed the entourage into the lobby and up these beautiful long stairs—Mother Teresa, then these big tall men, then her nuns, and then me at the end, like the errant little duckling in the Chinese story. We went into this big room packed full of all kinds of dignitaries—serious looking men, women in gorgeous saris. She spoke, and she was really tough and funny and not at all stiff or prissy as you'd think such a religious icon might be. She was amazing.

One person got up and said, "Well, Mother Teresa, they say it's better to teach people how to fish rather than just give them fish." She replied, "Most of the people that we work with can't even stand up, but I'll make a deal with you: I'll give them fish until they are well enough, and then you teach them." I was thinking, "Oh, this is kismet." Her talk ended, and they were about to take her off for some private reception. I flung myself past people at her, and she stopped and gently said, "What can I do for you?" And I babbled, "Oh, Mother Teresa, I want to come with you; I want to come to India; I want to be part of your order; I want to pick up dying people in the street, please, please. . . ." And she asked, "You need to do this?" And I said, "Yes, yes, I need to do this!" and I thought, "She understands me, she understands this hole in my heart that I need to fill." She gazed at me and she said, "No, you cannot come." I was devastated. The angels stopped singing. Everything became painfully real. I had been rejected by Mother Teresa! It was terrible. She didn't even know me and she rejected me. Then she looked at me and said, "When you are so filled with love for these people that you cannot bear to be away from them for another minute, then you can come." Just the implication of that was staggering! Here I was talking about my need, and it wasn't at all about that. I was crestfallen.

She asked, "What do you do?" and I answered, "I'm in the theatre," like confessing this horrible, paltry, putrid occupation. She smiled, nodded, and said, "There are many famines. In my country there is a great famine of the body. In your country there is a great famine of the spirit. That's what you must feed." Then she turned around and went into the reception room. Well, that kept me going for quite awhile, and still does.

Singing Is Not Enough

Contemporary worship is more characterized by passion. It has to do with the heart, with relationship, with an intimacy; it elicits feelings, emotion, tears, and intensity; it lacks substance. Worship needs both truth and passion. Truth without passion is dry. Passion without truth is empty. Where do we go to find both truth and passion? I suggest recovering worship as the proclamation and enactment of God's story.

— Robert Webber
The Divine Embrace

My friend Bruce lives by his hands. He is a skilled carpenter, accomplishing his beautiful work with efficiency; I am pretty sure he could build anything. He also uses those hands to play a mean guitar while leading worship.

Bruce is married to Adel, who is among the smartest people I know. Her smarts come with a water-tight memory—she does not forget a person, date or fact. She has her doctorate in education, and she is now a college professor.

Bruce is awfully smart himself, but he had an opportunity to get into the carpenter's union early, so he did not go to college. His self-deprecation in the face of his wife's accomplishments has become a comic aria that accompanies their relationship. He has now been taking college classes, so he is going to have to let that song go.

It was Bruce, Adel, Karen and I that made up a singing group called "Amos Endeavor." The group toured on weekends for about four years. We sang in churches and camps, and we focused on worship. The name we had chosen was our attempt to admit we were on dangerous ground. We knew, as reported by that ancient prophet, the Lord said,

> *Away with the noise of your songs!*
> *I will not listen to the music of your harps.*
> *But let justice roll down like water,*
> *righteousness like a never-failing stream!*
>
> (Amos 5:23–24, NIV, adapted)

We knew from other scriptures God was not opposed to singing as a worship activity. But we knew from that passage in the book of Amos worship and singing were not one and the same. Unless the leading edge of our worship was the rising wave of justice, we should not sing. Unless the river of holiness flowed through our lives, our instruments should remain unplugged and silent.

Who can live up to such a standard? Who has been never-failing in their justice and righteousness? Not I. I have known the clang of my heavy side of the scale hitting bottom. No perfection here.

All of us in Amos Endeavor knew we were not worthy worshipers, but there we were singing. We tried to explain at each of our concerts. I do not think we ever did a very good job, but we tried. We tried to say we did not think the Lord wanted to cut worship out of our lives. We struggled to explain that the words recorded in Amos gave us a worship image intertwining lament and praise, humility and boldness, confession and joy. Worship is thus a paradox, and we are ever and always helpless to complete this most sacred activity on our own. Grace is the key that opens the door to this sanctuary.

Those years are precious in my memory. Bruce, Adel and Karen became for me lifelong partners in this worshipful life which God has invited us to embrace. My attempt to live justly and rightly during those years was helped immensely by singing those songs over and over weekend after weekend.

After those four years, Karen and I moved so Karen could finish graduate school. More than two decades have passed since Amos Endeavor sang.

It was a few days ago that Adel e-mailed with the news Bruce nearly cut off his hand in an accident. He would be out of work for weeks, and he might never play guitar again.

Was this accident just? Was it good?

This past Sunday afternoon, we dialed their number. The four of us were soon talking and laughing together, sharing details of the accident and Adel's efforts to nurse this most impatient of patients—a man who would rather do anything than have someone do for him. He had just returned from another surgery that required the removal of nerves from his leg to place in his hand. He was now bed-bound, dependent on pain medication.

He quickly turned the attention away from himself, and we caught up on other details of each other's lives and children. Moments later we were stunned to discover they had quit attending the church that had been our home for five years and their home since they were children. Adel said, "I've never been divorced, but I imagine this is what it feels like. It's truly painful. And even though it has been almost a year, attending worship elsewhere still feels like cheating on a spouse." There have been other churches they have loved attending, but there is not a church that feels like home. Where do they belong?

They have not lost their faith. They are still longing to worship, but where, at their age? And what do they tell people who want to know where they have come from and why they left there?

Adel said, "I remember the moment. It was at a special business meeting. Our church was not doing well, and the pastor was struggling after two years of ministry. He said, 'Well, here are the statistics. As you can see, giving is down, attendance is down, and the facilities are suffering. I don't have a vision. What do you want to do?' I think he wanted to prompt us to take action for our church. There was a long silence."

Adel is one of the most methodical, reflective, disciplined and intentional persons you could meet. It did not surprise me to learn she had joined a professor colleague in a concentrated week of guided prayer that happened to fall immediately prior to this meeting. Was this combination of prayer and church meeting coincidence or providence? Did Adel's openness to God's voice impact what was to happen next? At the meeting, she raised her hand and said they had to look the difficult questions square in the face. Did they know their purpose? Was their role distinctive from other churches? If not, would it be better to collaborate with another church? She was getting at one of the toughest questions for a church to face. Is it time to close the doors?

The pastor said, "Those are good questions." There was a bit of discussion about evangelism as a purpose. Then someone said something like, "These are stupid questions. We shouldn't be talking about this. This is just stupid, stupid, stupid."

Adel had determined all those years ago she would follow God rather than worship itself. No specific time and place would become an idol. God was all there really was. And now she felt him saying to her, "There's your answer." In the silence after the last "stupid" she leaned over and whispered to Bruce, "I'm out of here."

I have known Adel many years, and she is more patient than her husband. Now I see there is an end to her long-suffering.

What is the last straw in such cases? Is it the lack of visionary leadership? Is it the unwillingness to face the difficult questions? Is it the injustice of cutting words that remain unaddressed? Surely Adel remembered the truth of Amos: "Where there is no justice, there can be no worship." But in this case, maybe "last straw" is not the correct metaphor at all. Maybe a better metaphor is God the surgeon gently removing a nerve from one place in the body and helpfully reassigning it to another place in the body, painful though that may be.

We had no answers for them. We did not tell them which church they should try. Their pastor had quit shortly after that meeting, and a new young minister is in the pulpit. Bruce said he feels too awkward to go back now since he is in such need of ministry himself. That is his personal curse.

Karen said, "We should pray." So we prayed for them, prayers affirming that we believe with all our hearts that God loves them and is healing and restoring them and is preparing a place for them. When they said goodbye, their voices were husky.

Our worship will never be perfect. And sometimes, the Lord cries, "Enough. No more singing now. There are other things that must be attended to." Such is not a time for despair. Such is a time for great endeavor, perhaps the greatest endeavor of all.

ADVENTURES IN
STORY AND WORSHIP

Stories Carry Hope

After Jesus was born in Bethlehem of Judea, during the time of King Herod, Magi from the east came to Jerusalem. . . .
— Matthew 2:1

Stories carry hope in their bones.

The congregation arrives at the church building with its own set of hopes, some of them admittedly selfish. "I hope we sing songs I like today. I hope the sermon isn't boring today. I hope we get out early today. I hope. . . ."

Then in a moment, someone stands and says,

> The trip so far had been a grand success. That night they went to sleep overjoyed. And one of the magi had a dream. More of a nightmare. He saw a shining being who spoke in a language that the wise man could understand. The shining being said, "Now that you have seen the child and delivered your gifts, go home." But the shining being made an additional remark. It said, "Go home a different road. Do not return to the king. He does not want to worship the child as he said. Get up and go home another way."

And then the music is playing and we are singing:

What child is this
Who, laid to rest,
On Mary's lap is sleeping?
Whom angels greet . . .

Do you see what has happened already? If we entered with any selfish hopes, they've likely been put on hold. We have thrown our interests in with those of the magi! Now we have new questions: Will the magi get home? Will they be safe? Will they follow the shining being's request? And what of the baby and the gifts?

Our story-hopes supersede our old, selfish hopes for the moment. That is the tremendous power of story in worship. Miss it, and you miss an amazing opportunity. An opportunity for focus, for peace, for joy. Misuse it, and you had better run, because now you have blown twice the number of hopes for this group of people.

Those who use story correctly will raise fascinating questions, and they will withhold the answers until just the right time. And they will connect any answers to follow-up questions. For example, "What Child is This?" is over and someone is saying,

The book that we love more than any other book tells us that the magi did not stay with the baby. They went home. They followed a dream and disobeyed a king. They went home by another way. And the king was very, very angry. Joseph, the husband of Mary, was asleep in his bed. And he, too, had a nightmare. "Wake up!" said the shining one. "Take the baby, take his mother. Run! Out of the country. All the way to Africa. Stop in Egypt. Wait for another dream. If you don't obey me, Herod's hench-

men will come, and you'll all be killed." Joseph was an experienced dreamer. He took his family, and they were gone like a whisper in the dark. But Herod didn't even bother looking for them. He just killed every single toddler in Bethlehem. He figured that was that. Little did he know.

And then maybe we sing a non-Christmas song, like this gospel song, and we sing it in 4/4 instead of 3/4.

> *Precious Lord, take my hand*
> *Lead me on, help me stand . . .*

Because story hopes are so satisfying, the old hopes—the admittedly selfish ones—are without their usual power.

Misunderstanding Worship

. . . my life is a story more than a list.
— Donald Miller
Searching for God Knows What

I have fallen into a lot of traps concerning the elements of worship. I am probably not so unusual. Worship is as tender and beautiful as haiku, so simple that it is impossibly complex, worthy of a lifetime of study.

For years I thought worship was our gift to God. Period. This idea was born out of my disgruntlement with worshipers measuring the success of Sunday by what they got out of it. I harrumphed, "Do you go to someone else's birthday party and come home upset because you didn't get a gift?" And so I swung hard the other way. Worship, to my new way of thinking, should be essentially a one-sided relationship. I came to think of worship as all about self-denial—giving, giving, giving to an infinitely worthy God to whom you could never give enough.

I forgot that we love God because he first loved us. I did not realize that my view of worship looked more like a stalking than a love affair.

Somewhere around this time in my development, a pastor invited me to help start a second morning service at his church. It was to be an experiment in worship style, so there were not strict perimeters. I asked him what he saw as being the necessary elements of this new service. He suggested we would have three simple elements: singing, preaching, and prayer. (He did not mention the announcements and the offering, which also turned out to be necessary.)

In my definition of worship, all the acceptable elements had to be outward toward God. Nothing inward (by which I meant "selfish") should be allowed. In this understanding, I could accept singing that celebrated and expressed love toward God, and I could accept preaching that called me to dedicate more of my life to God. But prayer did not fit. How, I wondered, could I worship God by asking him to give me what I, a selfish person, wanted?

Well, something had to change. Either I was wrong in my definition of worship or the pastor was wrong in asking me to include prayer in the design of the service. It turned out I was wrong, and I was wrong in more ways than one. Yes, my definition of worship was essentially heresy, leaving a gracious and loving God out of the relationship. But I was also wrong in my understanding of prayer. I guess I was imagining prayer was something I did on my own, something I would not call worship, some activity in which I would speak (either in my head or out loud) asking for stuff, and this stuff would be all my idea. The requests would basically be "gimmies," and therefore not worship (according to my now-understood-to-be-heretical definition of worship).

Consider this: If a prayer is not coming alongside what God is already willing and doing, then it might as well not be prayed. And if what I just said is true (and I now believe it is), then a prayer well-prayed is definitely a form of worship. Indeed, such prayer is saying "yes" to God.

I am going to be a lousy storyteller right now. I do not know when the change happened within me regarding prayer.

I do not know what caused it. I just know that I submitted to my pastor's desires for the elements of worship, and I changed.

Prayer became a major part of that second service—in fact it was the prayer time that was its most distinguishing feature. It was a time of unique openness, the closest our worship has gotten to that sense of an Alcoholics Anonymous meeting that I mentioned in the introduction to this book.

There was a guy who lived across the street from me who was a great electric guitar player. I knew little about his faith journey, but he played a jazz lick that was full of color and texture—he could wrap his fingers around that guitar neck and wring your heart out. I asked him if he would be willing to play in church, and he said yes. I invited him to join us at worship rehearsal. He said he would try. He did not show. But on Sunday he showed up just before the service, carrying his guitar and his own amp. And after that, he would sometimes show up on Sundays, carrying his equipment through that side door. I am not sure he ever showed up at a rehearsal.

I was not a very strict leader in his case. I was so overjoyed to see him in church that I did not recite him the rule, "If you don't show up to rehearsal, you can't play on Sunday." I would not recommend such laxness if you are a worship leader, but I did it anyway, taking a risk with gospel hopes. I do not know what happened to his soul on those Sundays. But he would sometimes show up. I would hand him an order of worship, and he would say thanks and set it aside and never look at it again. He just followed the mood in the room. Some would say he was Spirit led, but I do not really know. A twenty-minute song set was about all he could handle, and he would slip out the side door to have a quick cigarette break. His name was Brian.

I once asked Brian why he came to our church. I expected him to say, "Because it's the only church where I can play my guitar," and my letting him stay on the team would be immediately justified. That was not his answer. He said he liked the prayer time. It was the only time he had seen people be that vulnerable during worship.

Leap forward nearly two decades after I joined that pastor in helping start a second service. The church and I have both grown and continue to grow. This fall, we organized our first ever 24/7 prayer week. Our new senior pastor brought together a small team who agreed to pray, organize, invite others, and set up the sanctuary. The plan was to divide the week into one hour blocks and invite the members of the congregation to sign up for at least one hour to pray in the worship center. We had previously prayed for one day. We did that a few times. Then we prayed one week in which people signed up for a specific hour to be at prayer in their homes or at their work sites. Now we were ready to try for a week in the church building, in the place where we met together to worship. One of our team members said, "I think we should start smaller—maybe three days of twenty-four hour prayer." We thought for a heartbeat and said, "Nope. We're ready for a week. Here at church."

We created stations for prayer in the sanctuary. The stations represented the A.C.T.S. acronym for prayer: adoration, confession, thanksgiving, supplication. A small group of artists put together interactive visuals at each station.

The adoration station was near the piano with song books, books of written prayers, and a large wall of white paper with plenty of colored markers for making images as expressions of adoration. We were like kids making stuff for their mom or dad to put on the refrigerator—refrigerator art as worship.

The confession station was the communion table with a candle, a written prayer of confession, and a large white swatch of paper with charcoal for making marks in representation of sin.

For the thanksgiving area, Lois, who loves to do flower arrangements at our church, made a beautiful table decoration with fall flowers and gourds. Also on the table were various colors of Post-it notes for writing thanksgivings. The notes could be plastered on a large board which had been covered with black paper so the notes would visually leap like confetti. People coming to pray could join their spirits with thanksgivings already posted there, and then they could write and post some of their own.

The supplication station included pictures of missionaries our church supports, along with a basket to collect short written prayers for healing, salvation, or whatever. Someone listed our church leaders there to remind us that they need our prayers.

On the platform was an open Bible with a little Post-it marker. We were encouraged to find the marked spot and read aloud a chapter or two. We might be able to read through the New Testament in a week. There was a CD player with CDs scattered around for those who wanted music as they prayed.

During Sunday worship on the first day of 24/7 prayer, the stations were across the front of the sanctuary, with empty papers and unburned candles. As we walked out of worship, the week's prayers began. All that day, and the next, and the next, I would suddenly remember, "Someone is praying now." Surely this is always true. Surely the church catholic does indeed pray without ceasing. But this week was a more palpable reminder. These were people I had met and seen in church. And they were praying for many of the same things I was.

As I stopped by the building on Wednesday to check on the supplies, I saw that those papers were filling up with drawings, and charcoal markings and Post-it notes. I read the thanksgivings and saw the scrawlings at the confession table. I pondered the requests filling the basket. I saw a church full of people with passionate faith chasing after God. All those drawings and writings revealed a church that cannot be seen very often. Brian saw it when he showed up for the prayer in those experimental days of the second service. And here it was again. It was breathtaking and heartbreaking.

I signed up to pray at 3:00 in the morning. I was afraid I would oversleep, so my inner clock woke me at 2:15, long before my bedside alarm went off. I was glad I could turn the alarm off before it awakened my family. I crept downstairs. I was thinking about what I would find over at the church building when I got there. I hoped I would find one of my students, Tracey. I had talked three of my students into each taking one hour. I could not be certain whether they were doing it out of respect for the Lord or for me, but they said yes. I made some hot chocolate to give Tracey when I replaced her at 3:00. I think I was feeling guilty for urging a busy student to come alone to the church building in the middle of the night.

When I arrived, she was sitting on the steps at the front of the sanctuary. I wondered if she was asleep. I walked slowly up to her and began to say the Lord's Prayer, which was the way we had been instructed to pass the prayer baton. She was not asleep. I saw that she was writing in a prayer journal. She joined me in the prayer. As we got to "Give us this day our daily bread," I set the hot chocolate in front of her and she immediately reached for it. After we together said, "Amen." I said, "You may take that mug with you," and she said, "Ohhhh." She stood up and started to walk out of the sanctuary. Then she stopped and turned and said to me, "We should do this every week."

I do not know where our church's first ever 24/7 prayer week will lead us. But the week served to remind me that the story of the church at worship is always being lived. And every so often it can be seen.

Reclaiming Testimony

*"Thou shalt not" might reach the head, but it takes "Once upon
a time" to get to the heart.*

— Philip Pullman

Summer was coming up, and the worship committee had to
make a decision about what to do with summer worship.
The issue was: We could not fill two services during the summer.
During the school year, our church had two worship services
on Sunday mornings, each with a different structure and style.
But once the college students left town and families started their
vacation rhythms, the crowds thinned out, especially in the second service. At first we thought it was because the style of the
second service was not as preferred as the style of the first service. We came to discover it was more likely that people did not
want to be at church so late in the day on a summer Sunday.
They wanted to get to a picnic, or the lake, or the golf course.
So most people came to the first service, to the extent that the
second service was a motley crew.

The question came up, "Do we continue to have two services on Sundays during the summer, as we have for the past several years, even though the numbers are non-substantial in the
second service?" Normally, we would expect the pastor to make
a recommendation to the consistory (church board) about what
to do, but we were between pastors. So the issue came to the at-

tention of the worship committee. Why was the question brought up this year as opposed to previous years? You guessed it. Money. If we cancelled the second service and went to one service in the summer, it would mean we did not have to pay pulpit supply for two services.

It was pretty easy for the committee to agree to have only one service. Now came the tougher question. Which style? You probably need to understand this committee was not used to questions regarding the aesthetics or even the theology of worship. It met once a month and was charged with the pragmatics of worship—stuff like scheduling ushers and overseeing the annual worship budget, with line items including communion elements, advent candles, and of course, pulpit supply. This committee was not used to long meetings and a heavy workload. So they were ready to make a quick decision and get on with it.

Someone on the committee made a motion to form a sub-committee to answer this question. That motion quickly passed. Who would be on the sub-committee? (Are you enjoying this journey through church politics—maybe you have been there; it is more fun to watch someone else slog through than to do it yourself, is it not?) At this time in our church, the first service did not have a worship leader. The organist was essentially the worship leader. The service followed a set formula, and all the visiting preacher had to do was pick three hymns that went with his sermon. The rest of the first service would pretty much take care of itself. I was the worship leader for the other service. The tradition for that service was no one service looked very much like any other one. Are you getting the picture?

Back to the question as to who would be on the sub-committee to plan the style of the one summer service. They turned to me and said, "Jeff will you take care of putting together that sub-committee?" I said yes, and the meeting adjourned right on time.

I hope I have not been too glib or cynical in my reporting of this event. The worship committee members were good and concerned people, but they were also tired after a long day's work, and this new task was out of their purview. They were happy to let someone take the ball, and I was eager to avoid any micromanagement by such a large committee.

I solicited a mixture of eight people who were familiar with both of our usual services. I told them if they said yes, they must:

1. Be willing to meet once each week.
2. Be committed to pray for the services.
3. Expect to have a task to fulfill in preparation for each service.
4. Be an enthusiastic cheerleader for the summer worship series.

I told them their job would be done when we went back to two services.

We started our meetings in late April. The first summer service was in June. We met in the same place each week. It was the back screened-in porch of a consistory member. She welcomed us each week with homemade treats.

Every meeting included prayer. Several of us prayed each time. I asked specifically for prayers of gratitude and submission. I was not interested in a prayer time that devolved into polarizing prayers about which style God should bless. When we got around to asking for help from God, our prayers focused on people and their tasks.

Each meeting also included worship education. Not long, not complex, and not agenda driven. Principles that were scriptural and easily embraced. Worship theology creates worship unity. Every worship team meeting (and every worship service) is an opportunity for brothers and sisters to affirm why they are doing what they are doing. This requires vision and leadership, and it demands that we consistently return to prayer and the Bible. When we build this foundation, there is much hope.

Our planning team readily agreed we would not plan toward a first service style, or a second service style, or even a blend of the two. We set ourselves free to plan a new form we would simply call, "summer worship." And we agreed to communicate this in as many ways as we could to the congregation. We solicited a church member who was a graphic designer to help us with a large sandwich board that we put out in front of the church all summer long. And we put posters around the church and the town.

It was a lovely summer, and I remember it now with fondness. There was a good feeling in the place, and even the grumpiest did not complain. I suppose they just told themselves, "I guess I can wait until the fall. It's not that long."

As I look back on that summer, one incident stands out as a highlight. It was the day Jeanette told about God at work in her life.

Our committee had decided there should be something our congregation could come to expect throughout the summer. We decided upon a moment in the service that we called "God at Work in My Life." That was the phrase we printed in the church bulletin with someone's name next to it—each week a different name with a different three-minute story.

Certain worship traditions call this "a testimony." In our case, it would be planned, written and rehearsed, but it would still be a testimony. Other traditions call it a "witness." Maybe you have other terms for it, but we called it, "God at work in my life."

It was not such an "out of the box" activity for the second service congregation, but for many of the first service folks, it was pretty strange. They were used to a pastor and choir on the platform and seldom anyone else. Even if they did not oppose testimonies, such a thing was quite unexpected on a Sunday morning. The set aside nature of "summer worship" along with the repetition of this part of the service, however, helped this type of storytelling to be allowed and eventually even embraced by the congregation.

I gave very specific instructions to the dozen or so people who participated in this way through the summer. I told each person to be brief: two or three minutes. I gave them their first and last line. The first line was, "God has been at work in my life." And the last line was a phrase or sentence taken from scripture. I asked them to include some affirmation of the gospel of Jesus Christ. One sentence could be, "I'm grateful that Jesus died on the cross for my sins." Or it could be that the entire three minutes was their story of acceptance of the good news. Beyond these instructions, they were free to use the two or three minutes as they chose.

I asked them to feel free to attend Thursday night rehearsal to practice their piece with the rest of the worship team. If they could not, I asked them to send it to me in advance so I knew what to expect. My primary agenda was to get them to write it out. I encouraged them to memorize what they had written, but I gave them freedom to read it if they wished.

Once our planning team settled on this element of worship, we needed to figure out who to invite to help lead worship in this way. We started with a few of our own team members.

One day, in the middle of summer, on Marietta's screened-in porch, after we had prayed, we came to the question of scheduling the remaining people to share "God at Work in My Life." Someone said, "What about Jeanette?" I did not know her well, so I do not think I said anything. Someone else said, "She'll never do it. She's way too shy." Someone else said, "And softspoken." Someone said, "That's why we have microphones." Then it was Tom that said, "Let me do it. I'll ask her." And we nodded.

You should probably know Jeanette is a woman in her later years of life. Her career was spent as a nurse. Her husband died some years ago.

At the next meeting Tom excitedly told us about asking Jeanette to share. He had not called her on the phone but simply went to her house. He told her he had something to ask her and he did not want an answer that day; he told her he would come back the next day. He asked her to pray about it. And then he asked her to share her story in a "summer worship, God at work in my life" moment. I do not think he gave her any of the instructions. Not then. He would leave that for later.

The next day he went back to her house and told her he had come for her answer. Would she share in church how God had been working? She said, "Yes." He did not know why she said it. His guess was that she called one or two of her kids for their counsel. They were probably amazed she was considering it, and therefore, cheered her on.

I contacted her and went over the details. We were able to garner some family support by including some of her grandchildren on the singing team. It turned out her preacher son was available to be our pulpit supply that same day. Sunday arrived, and Jeanette was there very early to get her cue and practice at the microphone.

When the service started, one front pew was entirely filled with members of her extended family. When Jeanette stood at the microphone, the church fell unusually silent. Jeanette's story was written in longhand on half sheets of paper that she held in front of her the entire time. Her hands were shaking. Here is what she said, transcribed from the tape of that day:

> *As for me and my house we will serve the Lord. I am glad to have Harlan here and his wife Eunice. And I saw some other people here, relatives from California. I am glad to see you here.*
>
> *God is at work in our family. Many years have passed since I was born. I was raised in a Christian family, having two sisters and a brother. My parents have both passed away. My husband and I were married in 1941. Soon he was drafted into the army in 1943. We had two children at that time, and he was sent across in the European area. And we never saw him again for over two years. He was in a lot of action being in foxholes and a lot of gunfire. We were constantly in prayer and his life was spared. We had a happy married life for twenty-nine years.*
>
> *My husband had been struggling with a heart sickness. The service had been hard for him. As time went on the doctors thought surgery would be the answer. We prayed for guidance there, but he passed away in surgery. Many prayers were offered at that time. We had a prayer chain in this church when God chose to take him home. He was fifty-one years old.*
>
> *He left me with eight children—six sons and two daughters, and they were a challenge part of the time. (At this point there was much laughter in the church.) The oldest is Harlan and the youngest is Wes. The two oldest children were married at this time. Our oldest daughter was married three years and her husband was killed in a tractor accident. He left her with two children. My father was sick with cancer at this time and he too*

passed away. And this all happened in a year and a half's time.

[Here the tape is garbled for a few moments. She speaks of sending two sons into the armed forces during the Vietnam war.]

Their lives were spared through much prayer and always with God's help. He never left us nor forsook us. They were there in the service when their father died.

    Then nine years ago Wes was suffering with a kidney disease. His kidneys were failing in his teen years, but he never had to be on dialysis. As time went on we knew that he was failing so the doctors said he needed a transplant. So all the siblings were tested for a perfect match. Harlan was the only one of the eight children who matched. And it was a big decision not only for Harlan but also for his family and for Wes's family. With much prayer Harlan was willing to give his kidney. So when the day of surgery came, we were all in Rochester and many people at home and in our church here were praying again. It was hard to see two of my children go into surgery at the same time, but as they were taken away, I asked the Lord to take care of them. I was putting them both into his hands, and at that time, I felt peace within me, knowing that he would be with them. And they are both here today and doing well.

    We have had some anxious moments with the grandchildren too. One grandson died before he was born. A granddaughter was diagnosed with a muscle disease when she was a month old. But she had biopsies taken and many tests were done. We know our prayers were answered, and she is well today. Another granddaughter was very sick with a broken appendix, and a grandson who was seven years old needed surgery for a brain tumor. We prayed for guidance for the surgeons hands, and it was a delicate surgery. He is well today. One of our sons was very sick with malaria, and a son-in-law had extensive surgery to check for cancer. He is well today also. We know that miracles have happened in our family many times. And God has helped me, helped us through it all.

I felt a time that my prayers were not answered, but this is a trap of Satan. When I seem to have no answer, there is a reason. God uses these times to give me a deep personal instruction, and it is for me alone. I have gained patience through these hurts and afflictions. We have had many, many blessings also, not only hurts, but they are too numerous to mention. Many of the grandchildren have accepted Christ as their Savior. And we pray that the Holy Spirit will guide them and give each one a strong faith. Jesus gave his life for all, which was the greatest sacrifice. Let us give him all the glory and receive his forgiveness and mercy.

When she finished, I did not know whether to applaud or weep. I knew I had been in the presence of God's graciousness, and my heart nearly burst. She managed to fit the story of a faithful life in about the same amount of time it takes to sing a song.

You could ask a lot of people in our church about the summer Sunday that Jeanette shared about God at work in her life. I am guessing that those who were there still remember.

Stories as Pictures

We stood by the grave and sang, "Jehovah Jesus is my shepherd,"
after which Kuac took the Nuer translation of St. John's Gospel
from the back pocket of his khaki shorts and read the first few
verses of the 14th chapter. "The hut of my father has many
places. . . . The place where I go, you know the path to it."
— Eleanor Vandevort
A Leopard Tamed

Karen and I were once invited to speak at an annual missionary retreat in Wisconsin. It was not a large group, maybe thirty or so. Our assigned task, being college professors of theatre and speech, was to talk about communication. Not all missionaries are trained in public speaking, but they needed to travel to churches to share about their work. So we were given this rather open-ended task: help these leaders in their communication skills. We would have three or four hours spread over two days to complete the job.

I am not going to tell you precisely what we did for those three or four hours. I will tell you we had a lot of fun. We got them playing theatre games, we laughed and commiserated, and pretty soon we were treating each other like old friends.

Late in the afternoon of the second day, Karen and I somehow got the idea to have a missionary slide show. We thought this could be a time of building community—of sharing our mutual journeys of ministry in the service of Jesus. This slide show would bind us together and give us images to help us pray for each other when we left this retreat.

Of course, no one came prepared with pictures. So we asked them to create word pictures. We gave them specific instructions. We said to them, "Go back in your memory to a specific date, a specific time of day, a specific place, and a specific event that has something to do with your work as a missionary. Just stand at that place on that day at that time and look and listen. Write down what you see and hear. Be specific. Pay attention also to what you were feeling and write that down. Avoid the temptation to summarize or draw conclusions. Just be the camera or the tape recorder and show us what's happening around you and inside you."

We told them to be brief. Not to worry about complete sentences. We should be able to read their description aloud in about twenty to thirty seconds. We told them they had five minutes to finish the task. We probably cheated and gave them fifteen. But before long, they had turned in their papers, and we all went off to supper.

Before our evening gathering, Karen and I collated the images. We adjusted a few that were lengthy or preachy, but they were essentially as they had been turned in. We were delighted to discover you did not need names or dates to figure out which description belonged to which missionary.

That night we had the "slide show." Karen and I read them back and forth, with the change in who was reading serving as a cue the slide carousel had clicked forward to another person's image. We traveled around the world in fifteen minutes. We sat sipping hot chocolate by a Midwestern fireplace at the end of a wearying trip abroad. We stood on a school stage in India on graduation day. The image that sticks in my head and heart today takes place under a Tamarind tree in the Sudan. Here is what Roger Schrock wrote:

> *Nyadeng, a young disheveled Sudanese mother is paus-ing under a Tamarind tree in the early afternoon heat. She wearily supports her one-year old daughter on her left hip, and her right hand clings to her five-year old son. Tears stream down her face. There is no wind. Shim-mering heat rises from the dirt road in a wave of lonely lethargy. Behind Nyadeng, at the edge of the tree's shadow, is the carcass of an armored personnel carrier. Its door is ajar; its tires are flat. Patches of rust indicate that its life in the war zone is complete. But for Nyadeng, the horror of the war zone shall never die. Back up the road, she has just abandoned her three-year-old daugh-ter, who was too big to carry and too little to run. Nyadeng has left her, hoping to run fast enough and far enough to keep her two remaining children alive.*

I grew up before there was video or PowerPoint. I can re-member missionaries visiting my church and turning off the lights to take us to the faraway land where they worked. It was always fascinating—too slow, but still thrilling and formative of my faith. That night in Wisconsin was the best missionary slide show of my life.

Some images are best seen through word and story. What would happen if we regularly included such pictures in our wor-ship life together?

Story Pictures in Worship

... thy picture in my sight awakes my heart ...
— William Shakespeare
Sonnet 47

One fall at our college, I led some Saturday morning worship workshops. The hundred or so in attendance were a wonderful conglomeration of pastors, worship leaders, lay persons, and college students. I asked the attendees to write an image that represented a moment when they felt they were in God's presence. I gave them pretty much the same set of instructions that Karen and I gave the missionaries in Wisconsin—cite a specific day and specific time, describe what you see and feel, avoid telling us what to think about what you are showing us, and keep it very short (see previous chapter).

I told them that if they would turn their image in, I would consider using it in worship the next morning. But they had to be willing to let me use their name, and they had to be willing to let me edit their work. You might think I was foolish in waiting until Saturday to finalize this little piece of worship planning, but I wanted there to be a sense of immediacy to their writing. I was asking them to "write down the bones" (remember Goldberg's phrase from the introduction to this book?). I wanted the congregation on Sunday to scoot up as closely as they could to these mini-testimonies, knowing that they had just been written down the day before.

What follows is the set of images we used in worship that Sunday. One of the things you will notice is there is very little mention of God. Like the book of Esther in the Bible, it is the context that helps us discover the hidden One.

Linda, another member of the worship team, read these back and forth with me, fulfilling the function of helping the listener know we were moving to another person's image. In this case, we read the writer's name along with the image. The name lent authenticity. An added advantage in this case was most of these names were readily recognizable in our small town even though not all of these attended worship at our church. In one case, we added the writer's town since he was not from Orange City. (You might also notice that one of these stories re-appears in the next chapter. This is the way it works in communities; good stories bear repeating, and when they are repeated, the acknowledgement of the repetition cements relationship. Our culture unfortunately overlooks this advantage in its addiction to the new.) During the final image, the piano introduced the key and melody of a classic hymn, a verse and refrain of which we could easily sing from memory.

> LINDA: *Here are glimpses of the presence of God, written by some of those who attended the worship workshop yesterday.*
>
> *"April 14, 1994. There I was in a room full of other women, up in the mountains of southern California at a place called Twin Peaks. The speaker of the weekend, Terri, gave an invitation, asking us to simply look up at her to respond. I looked up."* Shelly Everson

JEFF: *"We watch our son running down a scree-covered mountain slope. No, not running. Too fast, losing control. Few ten-year-olds know this feeling on a 300 ft. mountain slope. Head over heels. Rag doll. Flopping. Turning. Stopped shy of the edge. Still. Carried down the mountain. Brought safely to rest. No injuries."* Shirley Folkerts

LINDA: *"My husband is dying. The nurse in ER says, 'He's out.' Within seconds, a team of medical staff is there. He is dead. But I feel a presence that gives me peace that I so much need at this moment."* Jan Wilbeck

JEFF: *"I was standing in a subway in Budapest. A little Hungarian lady came over and admired one of the Bibles. After some time, through the difficulty of language, I convinced her that I wanted to give it to her. She hugged the Bible, she hugged me, and went away."* Lynn Trapp

LINDA: *"'I was thinking about you today,' she says. 'I haven't heard from you in awhile; I miss hearing your stories about the events of your life.' Tears form in my eyes. She cares. My mom loves me. She asks me questions over the phone as she lies on the couch, wig on head, thin skin draped over bones."* Megan Hodgin

JEFF: *"She led me through the curtain. He was in his gown, chest shaved, IVs protruding everywhere, ready for surgery. I asked him how he was doing. His tough veneer cracked. 'It will be okay,' I told him. Then we prayed. He gripped my hand, not wanting to let go."* Pastor Brian Keepers, Sheldon

LINDA: *"Bob interrupts the band. We, thousands of kids, are all deathly still, for once. 'Chase's heart is in, and it is beating on its own.' The seated silence turns into leaping cheers. That was the one time in my life I cried for joy."* Hannah Barker

JEFF: *"He called home, a rare thing. With nervous energy and some tentative anxiety, he spoke of his experience. 'It was amazing, Dad. We prayed late into the night in the dorm lounge. I've never felt the power of God like this.' His prayers were the answer to mine."* Laird Edman

LINDA: *"We put in the video showing our new granddaughter. Tim appears, holding his baby. I look at Bill. Tears of gratitude stream down his face."* Sherri De-Boom

JEFF: *"Night. Quita and I walk, turning the corner onto Heritage Court. The dull orange of the streetlights. The distant garish glare of stadium lights. Wrapped in our own small thoughts. And there, just above the trees, the city, hangs the moon. A completely different luminance: soft, warm, sorrowful, watchful, silent."* Andy Sauerwein

The piano has gently begun, leading us to sing . . .

O Lord, my God, when I in awesome wonder
Consider all the worlds thy hands have made

Long Journeys of Faith

… only story can capture the dynamic interaction between humans learning to be partners and a God who calls and prods humankind toward partnership.

— Paul Borgman
Genesis: The Story We Haven't Heard

As I write this, our church is in our ninth or tenth summer of what we call "Faith Stories" on summer Sunday nights. The reason I remember that it has been nine or ten summers is because our current pastor arrived eight years ago, and it was one of the two summers we did not have a pastor that the worship committee came up with this idea.

The change took a bit of doing. I live in the conservative heartland where bookending a Sunday with two gatherings at the church building is a persistent tradition. Traditions, in such environs as ours, are like clothing—they are not discarded when go out of fashion but rather when they become completely worn out. The Sunday evening service was not yet threadbare, and so we expected it to continue.

When our previous pastor took a new call, our worship committee found a splendid interim preacher. Don was a passionate preacher, but he was recently retired. He was only willing to preach on Sunday morning, so our committee had to make other plans for Sunday evening pulpit supply.

In the midst of the discussion, someone came up with the idea to try something different. It might have been me. I often play the role of idea person on a committee, and then others have to scoot out the safety net. But in this instance, I do not remember all the details of the discussion. It was a good committee, and the ferment of best committees was happening that night. When that happens, it is tough for a single person to lay claim to the idea. No one remembers. It does not matter. This night was such a time, and the result of the evening's discussion was that summer Sunday evenings would no longer include a sermon. Instead, we would listen to the faith stories of one or two members of our congregation.

Before I explain the details, let me say again that stories are one of our greatest tools for remembering God. The God of Abraham, Isaac, and Jacob asked those ancient people to remember him as he would remember them. It was another way of expressing covenant. One of God's attributes is that he has no limit to his memory powers. If he wants to remember, he will. And even though our memories are not so perfect, God asks us to join him in that activity. He encourages us with simple tools, saying, "Remember! Write it down! In fact, graffiti the walls with it! Tell your kids; they'll help!" The concept of remembering is crucial to relationship with God. The word "remember" swings through scripture again and again like a clock's pendulum. God is saying, "I remember, you remember."

Our summer Sunday idea was doing good theology—the theology of remembering. Not "remembrance" as an idea. Remembering as an activity for living and relationship. Personal. Human. Messy. Organic. Alive. The kind of remembering that always begins with the word "I," as in "I remember when I was at Bible camp, thirteen years old, and. . . ." Even stories about a group event retain that personal quality. "I remember the Sunday morning that the candle wax ran down, and the communion tablecloth caught fire, and Glen was sitting right in front of me, and he got up from the front pew right while Pastor Jon was preaching. . . ."

Our committee included Ray and Dorothy. They were in their late sixties. I think they felt a bit radical that night, but they had been missionaries in the Middle East, so they were prepared to face opposition if necessary. They volunteered to be one of the first faith stories. That was what we needed—their gift of willingness. How could the rest of the committee say no to them?

The idea was that the worship service would still last about an hour. There would be an assigned host for the individual or couple sharing their faith journey. The structure of the evening would be:

1. Opening hymn—chosen by and especially meaningful to one of the people sharing.
2. Scripture—chosen by and especially significant to each of the people sharing.
3. Prayer by the host.
4. Introduction of person sharing.
5. Faith stories. The persons sharing were instructed to include their commitment to Jesus but also to include life details like where they were born, growing up years, getting married, major life events, and coming to this particular church. But they had freedom to shape the 45 minutes as they wished.
6. Questions from the congregation.
7. Closing prayer. During this time, the host invites two people to come and pray over the person or persons who shared.

That first summer, we had a dozen people share. We have not turned back since. Those Sunday nights are the best nights of the year. I have been amazed at what I have learned about the people I worship beside week after week. In a small and friendly community like ours, we all just sort of assume that we pretty much know each other. But who knew that the ebullient professional named John lived in a house with no running water when his mom brought him here from the Netherlands forty years ago looking for his dad who had run off with another woman? Who knew about the call in the middle of the night telling Marietta that there was a kidney available for immediate transplant and she should come now? Some knew these things, but a lot of us did not. Some of us have not lived here all our lives. And in a middle-sized church in a busy, busy town, we do not have time to hear such stories any more. We have to make the time. We even have to say no to some good activities to accomplish this great activity.

Here is an example. As I write this story down, I am remembering back to last Sunday night at my church, when Shirley and Rudy shared. Shirley played the piano that Sunday morning, as she often does. That night, she told us she had been sexually abused as a child. And Rudy told us of the terror of seeing his son falling down a scree-covered mountain slope, tumbling over and over like a rag doll. Rudy thought sure he was watching his son die. The emotion in that moment was so great it caused Rudy to cry as he remembered the image. But there sat healthy young Wade in the first row, smiling at his crying dad. Shirley and Rudy are relatively new to our church family. How many years would it have taken each of us in the congregation to hear these stories with the intensity and depth that they were told that night? It is most likely we would never hear them. Not without crafting the space and time and being very intentional in asking them to share their stories.

When we hear God's people tell their life stories in the presence of the gathered faithful, and we recognize the footprints of the Master, our hearts cry, "Oh! God!" Here is worship, in spirit and in truth.

Ancient Dramas of the Hebrew People

Apprenticeship to theatre includes apprenticeship to Scripture.
— Tom Boogaart

A couple of years ago, I received this email:

Hi Jeff,

Isaiah 5:11–12 reads:

"Ah, those who rise early in the morning in pursuit of strong drink, who linger in the evening to be inflamed by wine, whose feasts consist of lyre and harp, tambourine and flute and wine; but they have no regard for the deeds of the Lord, or see the work of his hands." [I am guessing this is Tom's own translation.]

What does it mean here "to see the work of his hands"? One way to explain this text would be that the people attend religious festivals, elaborate pageants that included sacred meals with food and wine, music with songs of praise accompanied by instruments, and dramatic per-

formances of the deeds of God. These people become so drunk that they do not pay attention to
the performances and thus do not "regard" God's
deeds or "see" the work of his hand.

Hope this helps,

Tom

Tom's email seems to be about an obscure little passage referring to a moment in Israelite history when some worshipers
were not paying attention to the performed stories about God's
deeds. But there is a story behind this interchange between Tom
and me.

Karen and I were on sabbatical from our professorships at
Northwestern College. We were guests at Western Theological
Seminary, team teaching a course in worship. I loved it. I got to
teach alongside Karen and also our dear friend Dr. Tim Brown,
one of the finest preachers I have heard. During our classes together, I came to discover that Tim is not only a great preacher,
he is also a great teacher. I became not only his fellow teacher,
but his willing student. I did not want the class to be over—it
was too good.

Near the end of our time together that fall, Dr. Brown
handed me an essay that one of his seminary colleagues had
written. "I think you'll want to read this," he said. As every great
teacher does with his or her students, Tim had figured out what
I was passionate about, and he was working to connect me with
like-minded scholars. So he handed me this nineteen page document.

I read the essay that night. It was an unpublished essay titled, "Drama and the Sacred." (Since that time, the essay has

been published in *Touching the Altar: The Old Testament for Christian Worship*, edited by Carol Bechtel.) The essay was by Dr. Tom Boogaart. The next day, I saw Dr. Boogaart in the seminary hallway. I called out, "Tom," and I came down the hall toward him. I said, "Tim gave me your essay 'Drama and the Sacred.' I read it last night, and I read it again this morning. I'd like to tell you what I think about it." And I knelt on the seminary floor and kissed Tom's shoe.

Sure I felt silly. But I wanted to say to Tom that something terribly significant is going on. And when you want to say that something terribly significant is going on, it is time to use drama. So I got on the floor and kissed Tom's feet.

What was the big deal? What was in those nineteen pages?

Well, pick up these two books: a theatre history book and a Bible. Tom says what the first book says about the second book is wrong. The theatre history book will tell you the first playscripts in history emerged from Greek culture. Tom says that playscripts written long before the Greeks are found in the second book, the Bible. Theatre history books typically say ancient Israel had no theatrical tradition. Tom says ancient Israel had a rich theatrical tradition, and we have the plays to prove it.

At first glance, this is not a new idea. Many have thought of the dialogues in the book of Job as dramatic. Some scholars have also argued that various prophets have affirmed the power of drama by enacting metaphors. Like Hosea marrying Gomer—performance art on a grand scale. But Tom is asking us to consider a much larger chunk of the Bible—a broad swath of stories that use dialogue and action—from Genesis to Esther. The first half of the Hebrew Bible is, says Tom, a play anthology.

Tom's essay stunned me. I could hardly believe it. If this is true, it changes the way we think about the Bible. And about theatre history. And about worship. As a worship leader and also as a professor of theatre, I have often dealt with questions like, "Where in the Bible does it say that drama is a worthy activity? Where in the Bible does it say that drama and worship have anything to do with each other? Where in the Bible does it say it's okay for a gifted young theatre artist to spend time and money developing his or her skills?"

I have taken those questions seriously, and I have what I think are pretty good answers. But if the Bible contains plays, then the answers become self-evident. And if God's plays are going to be performed with excellence, well . . . then, we need theatre majors.

But I had to slow down. I first had to wonder how I had missed this idea. How could I have been reading all these plays and not know they were plays? What was Tom seeing that I had missed all these years?

I asked Tom if we could talk more, and he invited Karen and me to his house. I learned a bit more about him. Dr. Boogaart is a Hebrew scholar, having studied in the United States, the Netherlands, and Israel. He is in love with the Bible. He says its craft and beauty take his breath away. And he is in love with the God of the Bible. He is a person of prayer and worship. He is a preacher. And he is a scholar who works with care and methodology. His white beard is carefully cropped. He moves slowly. He smiles gently. He speaks softly.

Tom and Judy prepared a wonderful meal for us in their beautiful older home situated on a diagonal street that cuts across the south edge of downtown Holland, Michigan. They gave us carefully prepared hors d'oeuvres and iced tea. I wish you could spend an evening having dinner with Tom and his wife. I wish you could have a long conversation and ask all your questions. I will try to summarize for you, as best I can, what

Tom told us.

What Christians call "the Old Testament" and what Orthodox Jews simply call "The Bible" is a collection of a variety of kinds of writing. You probably know this fact. It includes laws, census data, mystical future telling, and passionate sermons. It also includes art. It has songs and poems and elaborate descriptions of architecture and sculpture. So far so good. But what the book is mostly made up of is stories. These are stories based on history. Stories with structure: a beginning, middle and end. Stories with conflict: a problem, a struggle, and a resolution. Stories with characters who speak in dialogue. That last fact is often overlooked, so let me assert it again. The vast majority of stories from Genesis through Exodus are told using dialogue and narration.

Here is where I was in my personal journey as I sat in Tom's house. I could believe these stories emanated from an oral and largely illiterate culture, and thus they would have been kept alive in that culture by some sort of performance tradition. It was also likely these performances were a part of feasts or other worship events in that ancient culture. Tom reminded me, though, the Israelite culture did not have any of the sacred/secular distinction that some of us have today—all of life truly was worship.

"What were the performances like?" I asked Tom. He told me we do not know. We have to remember that most of the clues about that culture are contained in the pages of scripture. We have to extrapolate from there. "Where might they have been performed?" I asked. "Were there theatres?" Tom explained we are looking back at a civilization that faced dislocation and virtual annihilation. Again, we must look at the Bible.

Okay. I can accept that the Bible contains texts of what were once live performances of stories at some sort of worship event. But I am a theatre artist, and more specifically I am a playwright. Theatre people draw a distinction between storytelling and acting, between the literary form called "story" and the literary form called "drama." I asked Tom about this distinction, and he sort of threw up his hands and said, "Well you know more about that than me." He was basically saying, "Does it really matter?"

That was pretty much where I ended that first night at Tom's house—no clear certainty that we were looking at plays rather than stories. To Tom this distinction did not matter so much, but to me it mattered a great deal. If I was going to suggest to theatre historians that there was a whole body of dramatic literature that they were overlooking, I had better be prepared to justify my case using the technical distinctions of our art form.

Do you know what I am talking about? How can I help you understand the distinction? For something to be a play, it needs an actor representing a character in action in front of an audience. Theatre is an art form that brings the audience into a dramatic present—it is not the past anymore. We are here with the event—it is live, onstage in front of us. It is not someone telling about something that happened in the past. It is about someone showing something that is happening (metaphorically) right here right now. I was not certain that what Tom was calling the plays of the Bible were really shows. They could be *tells*.

The fact there are characters saying lines does indeed seem to move these stories over into drama. For example this line spoken by an Assyrian King: "In such and such a place shall be my camp!" Character, dialogue, live in front of an audience. Sounds like acting to me.

But I had to wonder about the narrative voice in each of

these stories. All of the narrative voices in the Bible stories speak in the past tense. This distinction is a typical way to separate a story from a play. Stories are usually past tense, and plays are almost always present tense. If there is a play with a narrator, then the playwright will usually work to get that narrator to the present tense whenever possible. I write a lot of plays with narrators, so I worry over such things. Here is an example from one of my own plays, *September Bears*, a play set on 9/11.

> SUE
> I don't know why we had school that Thursday. But we did.
>
> (Children enter, standing for the pledge.)
>
> SUE (continued)
> I guess we thought the routine would help. So I give Daisy our dog a goodbye rub, make the drive from Manhasset to Manhattan, arrive at school, welcome the children, stow the lunch boxes, binders in desks, pencils sharp. Just like every day.
>
> (Children put their hands on their hearts.)
>
> SUE and CHILDREN
> I pledge allegiance to the flag.

Did you see the switch from past tense to present tense? This switch is where the story becomes a play.

We know the Bible contains stories. And we have a very strong sense that these stories were once performances of some kind. Were these performances of stories or were these performances of plays?

Listen to the beginning of this story from 2 Kings 6. "Then the King of Syria warred against Israel." That sounds like the past to me—a story. Where is the dramatic present? If it is past tense, it seems like some sort of pre-theatre storytelling form, not actually theatre.

A month or so after I kissed Tom's shoe, I went on a trip to Japan with my church. A seventy-year-old Japanese man named Hiroshi took my family and me to the Kabuki-Za in Tokyo. We watched a Kabuki play, an ancient theatrical form. Kabuki has fascinating conventions, including the fact that all the women characters are played by men, just as in Shakespeare's day. I noticed that during the play the actors would sometimes speak their lines and sometimes sort of sing them. It could hardly be called realism. There was also a performer who sat off to the side, singing a great deal. After the performance, I asked my Japanese hosts about the singer off to the side. "Oh," they said, "That's the narrator." "What's the narrator singing?" I asked. "Well, they connect the parts of the story together and sometimes tell us what the character is feeling." I immediately began thinking about the narrator in the Bible stories. So, I asked my hosts to tell me if the narrator in Kabuki was singing in present tense or past tense. They looked at me curiously and said, "Your question doesn't make a lot of sense with the Japanese language. It's pretty much the same."

When I got back to the States, I asked Tom, "The narrative lines in ancient Israelite dramas, in the Hebrew, are those present tense or past tense?" Tom said, "Your question doesn't make a lot of sense with Hebrew. It's pretty much the same." Then I stumbled upon *Young's Literal Translation*, a version prepared in the late nineteenth century. The point of Young's version is to make verb tenses match between Hebrew and English. So, for example, when the King James says, in 2 Kings 6,

> *Then the King of Syria warred against Israel and said unto his servants . . .*

Young's says,

> *And the king of Aram hath been fighting against Israel, and taketh counsel with his servants, saying . . .*

Do you see what has happened? The English translators have looked at the narrative voices in Hebrew and said, "Oh, it's a story—so in our culture that should be translated past tense." But they could have said, "It's a play, so that should be left in present tense, because that's what plays do." Maybe this difference does not matter to you, but it matters a great deal to people who write theatre history. And it matters a great deal to the theatre artists of the world.

At the college where I currently teach, theatre is accepted. The most expensive building that my college (a Christian college) has built to date is the new theatre complex containing two theatres to support an energetic and vital theatre program. Theatre art is affirmed where I work. But not all of my students come from families and churches that embrace their artistic gifts. And many of my Christian theatre colleagues from around the country operate in schools, churches and communities where their life's work is constantly challenged.

Think about it this way. What if you opened the Bible to read Psalm 150. And instead of saying to praise him with trumpet and guitars and drums and organs, what if Psalm 150 said,

> *Praise the Lord! Praise God in his sanctuary. Praise him with monologue and dialogue. Praise him onstage, backstage and down in the pit. Praise him in the booth, on*

the headset, in the green room, dressing room, box office,
coat room. Praise him with scenery and lights, costumes
and props. Praise him with laughter and tears, from Act
one, scene one until "Ring down the curtain!" Let every-
thing that breathes praise the Lord! Praise the Lord!

What if it said that? And then, what if there were no explicit
mention of music in the Bible? What if there were not a single
song lyric printed anywhere in the book? Imagine what musicians might be told? "Since there are no songs printed in the
Bible, music and worship don't go together. Playing instruments
is a waste of time, impractical, even immoral—it's associated
with the world—it's not for the church."

Do you see why I got on the floor and kissed Tom's feet?
Plays in the Bible.

I had become convinced Tom was right. So immediately
after our sabbatical, I went to work with my touring company,
trying to present some of the oldest scripts in the world. We
were not adapting biblical texts. We were attempting to perform
precisely what we found. We were reclaiming something lost.

With Tom's help, we chose a short play from the book of
Kings and gave it a title: *The Bands of Syria.* Our team worked
to develop a simple set of theatrical conventions. We chose King
James because the language of that translation immediately reminds modern audiences that these plays are neither realism
nor are they contemporary. We received assistance and feedback
from Dr. Joonna Trapp, Northwestern scholar in pre-literate
cultures, and Dr. Robert Hubbard, Northwestern scholar in
theatre history and performance studies. I also consulted with
our college's Old Testament and Hebrew scholars, Dr. Jim
Mead, John and Kathy Brogan, and Dr. Syl Scorza. The performers and I convened in Virginia, with Dr. Boogaart, at the

Christians in Theatre Arts national conference to share our discoveries and investigate some other Bible plays. Our work was affirmed in this surprising way. We were leading a workshop with a group of directors from around the country. We were watching a director attempt to stage a version of the burning bush text. God tells Moses to take off his shoes. The director said, "Stop. Moses, you should take off your shoes." The actor obeyed the director, but we all realized in that moment that the Bible never says whether Moses obeyed. An artistic choice must be made, and a performance immediately makes clear what a reading leaves vague. The rehearsal continued and the actor playing God told Moses what was going to happen to him, and then he told him to get going. So Moses exited, and Tom leaned over and said to me, "Look! He left his shoes." On the last day of the conference, the play was performed for the workshop class, and that bit of business remained—the shoes were left behind—a powerful reminder of Moses's obedience and changed life. And a powerful reminder that there is so much to be discovered in any play when you stop reading and put it on its feet.

When I returned from Virginia, I found this note waiting for me from Tom:

> *What a moving experience it was to see* The Bands of Syria. *I have worked with texts like this for a long time, and in doing so I had to imagine how it might have looked to the people of Israel. The text suggested a performance, and imagining the performance helped me to "see" the text. But . . . seeing it, really seeing it . . . I was not prepared for the impact that it made on me. It is not enough to read texts and imagine, we need to perform them. And this is not just true for me, it is true for everyone in the church.*

By the time of this writing, we have created two full-length musicals which are collections of stories directly from the Bible. Our first musical is called *And God Said*, with original music by Broadway composer Ron Melrose. The second one, a collection of some of the more troubling stories in the Hebrew Bible, is called *A Holy Terror*, with an industrial rock score by Joseph Barker and Heather Josselyn-Cranson. We have also produced several versions of *David and Goliath*, as well as a collection of Elisha plays and several stand alone dramas. (*The Bands of Syria* is included in the appendix section of this book.)

One of the beautiful moments in this journey was when we staged the Abraham and Isaac story. There is Abraham above his son with the knife raised in the air. When Abraham is told to stop, he sees a ram, which he offers instead of his son. When you stage this scene, Abraham has to remove Isaac from the altar before he can get the ram. The most efficient move that presents itself is to have Abraham quickly cut Isaac's bindings. When Tom saw our staging he said, "Jeff, that's one of the more common gestures in scripture—that which was intended for destruction is used for redemption." Did we invent that gesture, or was it waiting to be revealed the moment the text was turned into action?

If what Tom says is right, then a worldwide movement will occur. These ancient plays will move from the page to the stage. Things will change in the culture. Theatre artists everywhere will no longer be able to say that they have studied theatre history until they have also studied the Bible.

And things will change in the church. It will no longer be enough to read these passages aloud in worship. The acknowledgement that we have dramas in our most sacred text will mean that every worship community will craft playing spaces, will invite actors into those spaces, and will design worship services to include performances of these ancient plays that show the deeds of the Lord.

This Play Is Based on a True Story

ARLENE
Today is the Sunday afternoon service that will stand out from every other Sunday afternoon service in my young life. It's a normal 1:00 service. We're into the sermon. The text is Isaiah 6:8. "And I heard the voice of the Lord saying, 'Whom shall I send, and who will go for us?' Then I said, 'Here am I, send me.'"
 (Beat.)
I don't know how to show you. Maybe just use your imagination. In a moment, you might see it.

FEMALE #4
Imagine inside an old church building,

FEMALE #5
Old pews.

MALE #3
Big organ pipes.

MALE #1
And a high gallery that wraps around.

FEMALE #2
And there's a young woman sitting there on a pew in the gallery.

ARLENE
She's me.

— Sioux Center Sudan

There is a reason this chapter follows the previous one. The reason is simple. I especially want you to consider these two types of drama within worship:

1. Scripture stories.
2. True stories from contemporary life.

The previous chapter was about the former. This chapter is about the latter.

Just in case you are reading the chapters of this book out of order, or in case I have not been plain enough, let me underline that I am not suggesting that every Bible story and every true contemporary story should be acted out. Much of this book is about reclaiming the simple power of storytelling. Emphasis on simple. One person, stand up, tell the story, sit down. Tremendously powerful. Extra spectacle can get in the way and diminish that power. Please—pretty please—be careful.

But sometimes, the artists of the church become convinced their more elaborate skills are being requested. Do not ask how artists know this, but we do. How does a woman know it is nearing time to give birth—she gets kicked in the gut! That is what we artists feel, a kick in the gut. We cannot prove it to you, but we feel it and have to respond. Here is a story about a time in my life when I felt that kick in the gut.

A few years ago, at a summertime theatre conference, I was sitting at a performance of *Early One Morning* (Ron Melrose's one-woman musical about Mary Magdalene—talk about elaborate crafting—whew!). I turned to Lin Sexton who was sitting next to me, and I said, "This is too beautiful." I meant it. I felt that I was sitting in—breathing—beauty.

Lin replied, "You need to feel called by God to write a play about the civil rights issue of our time."

That seemed to me like a non sequitur. What in the world did she mean? Turns out, she was speaking in the way that prophets sometimes speak. Forget your agenda, they have something on their mind. Lin was speaking of justice for the women in the church. She was saying that the women's rights movements of the twentieth century saw this one particular group of women and passed by on the other side, leaving them to their own defenses. She was suggesting that such a complex issue could be served by the careful crafting of a work of art. Lin has seen and appreciated some of my own writing for the theatre. When she heard me speaking of beautiful writing, she thought it might be time to address her own agenda.

I felt a bit like a prophet of another sort—Jonah—a prophet who heard a call and went the other way. I had already heard words like Lin's from my wife Karen and my colleague Joonna, but I had not yet put pen to paper. I had gone to Tarshish. Lin's voice was reminding me of the state of things in Nineveh.

How do artists start projects? They have many different ways. Some get up every morning and work in a set place for a set period of time. That discipline is their protection. A specific place and time keeps them headed in the right direction, like the banks of a river keeping a river on course.

I am a different sort of artistic personality, so that river comparison does not work for what I do. I need more pressure. Life is too interesting, and the search for knowledge and inspiration (the research part of a project) has no end at all—that wheel spins forever. So I need something to confine me. I am like Jonah—I need to get thrown overboard and swallowed by a great fish. There, confined in the fish, the work gets accomplished. How does it happen? Well, it started for Jonah with a confession: "We're in this storm because of me, and nobody can take care of it except me, so throw me overboard."

I have to have a storm. It provides the urgency to take decisive action. What it usually means for me is an impending performance date. That creates the storm. The storm will not subside until I go over the side into the fish and finish the work. My fish is my upstairs office. The screenwriter William Goldman calls his office "the cave," but he means the same thing as "the fish." It is a desolate, confining, lonely place. Such a place is not easy for anyone involved, not for me, or my family, or my friends. I would rather be at the movies, or at dinner, or sleeping, but I have to go into the fish, and I will be back when the work is done. The first part of every voyage is peaceful and pleasant, but there will come a storm followed by a great fish. Ask Karen.

So back to Lin's prophetic urging. I told her I would keep it in mind. I returned to school that fall and cast my touring theatre ensemble. I did not have a play, but there was a storm on the horizon. On a certain day in February we would leave on tour. I told my ensemble I was going to attempt to write a play for them about the civil rights issue of our time. They trusted my track record, so they were willing to wait. Months went by. I knew I wanted this play to be based on a true story. My reasoning was audiences in the context of church would feel less preached at, less manipulated if they knew they were watching a piece of someone's real life. In addition, the fact that the incidents have been lived tends to make it less easy to brush their reality aside. It seems to me that there tends to be more respect for the characters. So I was looking for a woman whose story I could tell.

That fall, Carol Anderson, a Christian and actress from North Carolina, came to speak and perform at our college. She visited our touring company rehearsal to swap stories of life on the road. That day's rehearsal happened to be held on the set of

Sky Girls, a play by Jenny Laird about women pilots in World War II. When we told Carol that we had decided our next project would be a true story of a woman in ministry, she looked down at the airplane wing she was sitting on and said, "Maybe you should do a play about Betty Green. She was one of the co-founders of Missionary Aviation Fellowship. When she used to fly into the Sudan, the air traffic controllers were so surprised to hear a woman's voice that they gave her the nickname, 'The Golden Voice of the Sudan.'" So, I started researching Betty Green.

A few weeks later, during the run of *Sky Girls*, a tall white-haired woman was sitting behind my wife Karen, who was the director of the play. At intermission she said, "Are you Karen Barker?" Karen nodded, and the woman said, "When I lived in the Sudan, I knew a sky girl. Her name was Betty Green." Bingo. Karen listened eagerly until the lights dimmed to end intermission, but then in the hubbub after the play, the woman was gone. Karen never got her name.

The next day at rehearsal, I said to my touring company, "Karen met a tall white-haired woman who knew Betty Green in the Sudan, but we have no idea who she is. I only know that this woman lives in Sioux Center." One of our actors, Matt, said, "That sounds like Arlene Schuiteman. She goes to my home church. She's in her eighties now, but she was a missionary in the Sudan. You should meet her. She'll change your life."

By now, it was almost Thanksgiving. I knew I would need several weeks "in the fish" and then we would need about a month to rehearse. I was almost out of time for choosing a topic. The storm was about to begin. I asked the touring company if they were still committed to my writing this play. We went around the table. Most of them were keeping their options open, but one young woman said, "I want to work on a new script. I want you to write this play." It was the encouragement I needed, so I promised the company that I would try to speak with Arlene over the Thanksgiving break, and then we would make our decision.

I called Arlene, and she agreed to meet me. We sat at her kitchen table, and she told me what she knew of Betty Green. Then, as I continued to ask questions, she gradually unfolded her eight years as a missionary nurse among the Nuer people in the south Sudan. She told me of the annual cycle of flood and drought and the permanent state of disease. She told me of snakes and spiders and reverence for cattle. As she talked, I was getting a suspicion I had found my play. She told me of the day she received a telegram expelling her from the country. It was the same week that President Kennedy was shot. She never went back to the Sudan. It was one of the greatest heartaches of her life. Then she told me of the day Sudan returned to her. She had gone to a worship service in Sioux Falls, South Dakota. A large group of Sudanese refugees—fleeing civil war and genocide—had wound up there, of all places. Someone had discovered Arlene knew the Nuer people, and she was invited to come and worship. She went. A woman preached, and after the sermon, Arlene was invited to stand and introduce herself. "My name is Nya Bigoaa," said Arlene, using her Nuer name. A man came over to her and said, "Nya Bigoaa John? I am the son of your friends. We have heard about you all our lives."

Kick in the gut. And a strong wind began to blow.

I asked Nya Bigoaa if she would let me write a play about her. She said she would, as long as I did not put her on a pedestal. And then she went up into her attic and pulled down a box labeled "Sudan things: Needs sorting." It was a gold mine, and she handed it into my care. I went overboard and into the fish.

The result was *Sioux Center Sudan*. In the process of that journey, my students had to study African culture and learn some of the Nuer language. Best of all, they met and became friends with Arlene and her fellow missionary, Eleanor Vandevort (also called Vandy), and read Vandy's wonderful book *A Leopard Tamed*. Who knew such a treasure was waiting to be discovered just twelve miles away!

We took the play on tour, ending that spring with a performance in the church that had nurtured Arlene throughout her life. That night the church was jammed with over a thousand people. A drama can generate electricity and invitation. That night was an event.

Vandy (also in her eighties) had flown in from Pennsylvania. Dr. Bob Gordon, Arlene's Sudan medical supervisor, was brought by his son from his retirement village on the other side of Iowa. Several Sudanese natives had traveled from as far away as Georgia.

One Sudanese man stood up after the play and said, "I want you to think of the most famous movie star you know. Think of what it would be like to meet that person. That's how we feel being here tonight and meeting Nya Bigoaa and Nyarial (Vandy's African name). And Dr. Bob. We have heard about them all our growing up years. We are Christians today because of what they did for us."

In one more way I was like Jonah. I had started out with a specific prophetic message for the church, but God had his own agenda. This play was no longer about the civil rights issue of our time. I told Lin that I would have to try again. This play was about . . . well, I do not know how to put it in a sentence.

I can say that Arlene and Vandy had an experience that many people do not ever have. They lived to glimpse the other side of the tapestry—to see connections between what God was up to at places and times separated by continents and decades.

The end of our own story is never ours to write. We each have been assigned another part in the plot of our lives—the part called *faith*—to believe God not for what he would do, but for who he is.

This Is Not the Real Story

Now the moment of prayer for me—or involves for me as its condition—the awareness, the re-awakened awareness, that this "real world" and "real self" are very far from being rock bottom realities. I cannot, in the flesh, leave the stage, either to go behind the scenes or to take my seat in the pit; but I can remember that these regions exist. And I also remember that my apparent self—this clown, or hero or super—under his grease-paint is a real person with an off-stage life. The dramatic person could not tread the stage unless he concealed a real person: unless the real and unknown I existed, I would not even make mistakes about the imagined me. And in prayer this real I struggles to speak, for once, from his real being, and to address, for once, not the other actors, but—what shall I call Him? The Author, for He invented us all? The Producer, for He controls all? Or the Audience, for He watches, and will judge, the performance?

— C. S. Lewis
Letters to Malcolm: Chiefly on Prayer

Our college drama team led a workshop this past week about an image prayer form we pray. We call it *enacted prayer*. As part of the workshop, I asked if anyone in the audience of seventy or so had a personal praise or request that they would be willing to share with us. A woman near the back raised her hand. She said, "I'm praising God that the day my daughter found out she was pregnant she quit using crack cocaine."

We joined this praise by acting it out. I simply asked my drama team, "Who will play the daughter? And the mom? And who will represent God at work in this situation?" Then I said a couple of things about the actors who represent God. I said that we were not trying to make any point about the gender of God. And I pointed out that the actors representing God were putting sashes around their necks just so we can all remember they are standing in for God and not people. Then I asked an actor to stand in for someone who had been providing the daughter with drugs. And I asked an actor to represent a doctor. And another actor to represent the unborn baby! Then just before we began the prayer, I had another idea. I said to one of our actors, "Lindsay, want to play crack?" She grinned and blurted out, "Heck, yeah!" Her word choice caught me off guard, but I knew she had no intention to offend. I promptly cast her in the non-human role of an addictive drug, and so the prayer began.

The actors took the story back to a time when the daughter and her friend were still involved in using drugs. And then, she felt sick. And she went to the doctor. We saw her mother praying for her. We saw her unborn baby being formed. And throughout this, we could see God moving in and among the people, mysteriously and powerfully. We could also see Lindsay with her arms around the daughter, like a desperate lover. And when the doctor told the daughter she was pregnant, she turned to her friend and said something we could not hear—indeed, no words are actually spoken in this prayer form, and music plays from beginning to end. The friend got the picture and fled. God confronted Lindsay, and crack fled to the departed friend. The daughter sat on a stool, God brought her baby to her embrace, and the mother joined the embrace. They all froze in an instant picture of praise for that which had been accomplished, we believed, with God's help. Mother, daughter and grandchild

were alive and well and free. As the image burned into our imaginations, I finally said, "In the name of Jesus we pray, amen." The
set up took about three minutes, and the prayer itself took two.

It feels so clunky to attempt to capture this prayer on
paper. I guess a picture really is worth a thousand words. I
turned to look at the mother who had requested the prayer, and
she was mopping her face with the back of her hand. She was
not the only one. After about ten years of witnessing enacted
prayers, I can attest to the instant power of this prayer form.

Why should these simple and brief prayers carry such
power? I am not sure. But here is my guess. Seeing a picture of
what we are praying affirms what C. S. Lewis wrote to Malcolm:
". . . this 'real world' and 'real self' are very far from being rock
bottom realities." Enacted prayer lets us glimpse into the rock
bottom reality of being in God's presence. And that rock bottom reality is so beautiful it makes us weep. Can it be true? Can
it be that God was already at work before we prayed? We
quickly realize that our answer is yes. We could not quite have
put our groaning into words, but we recognize it when we see
it.

This form of prayer began for us in 1995 when we were
using Jo Salas's book *Improvising Real Life* to create a new show
for our company. Jo's book tells about a form of theatre in which
an audience member tells a story or dream and then the players
act it out. One day while we were praying before rehearsal, we
prayed for a man in our church who was desperately ill in the
hospital. We prayed that God would go to his room at the hospital and heal him and return him home to his family. Suddenly
we realized that we could easily create an image of our prayer
by acting it out. We did, and the prayer took on a more vital reality for us. At that time, I was worship leader at our church, so
I asked the team if they could enact the same prayer in the serv-

ice on Sunday. Our church has always made room for spontaneous prayer about congregational concerns, so the groundwork had been laid.

The enacted prayer on Sunday was again vitally real, and our friend and his family were grateful for it.

A new adventure in prayer was begun. In the following months, we continued to experiment with praying in this way. Our experience was that the images of these prayers made them not only moving but memorable. All these years later, I can recall from that first year a drama workshop in which we prayed for a broken relationship in a household within the church. I recall a Sunday School class in Wisconsin where we prayed for the family of a woman who had just been tragically killed in a construction accident. I recall a pastor's conference where we prayed with a pastor whose parish was filled with single parent homes. In each case, the prayers were simple, vital, and strangely moving.

Since that first year, we have used this form to pray spontaneously in groups from two people to two thousand. We have presented enacted prayer workshops at several conferences, and a few theatre groups scattered across the globe have begun to join us, from California to New York to Singapore. It is slow going because until people see this form or try it themselves, they remain skeptical.

We have sensed the Spirit of God working among the theatre artists of the church, and we believe this prayer form is one of the many results of that work. And we have seen the value of this work, especially as it reminds us (in the words of C. S. Lewis) that "this 'real world' and 'real self' are very far from being rock bottom realities."

Why Things Happen

As he went along, he saw a man blind from birth. His disciples asked him, "Rabbi, who sinned, this man or his parents, that he was born blind?"

"Neither this man nor his parents sinned," said Jesus, "but this happened so that the work of God might be displayed in his life."

— John 9:1–3

Our drama team was invited to perform at a national conference for women. We were assigned to perform the play *Sioux Center Sudan* in a large banquet hall after a nice dinner. Then our assignment began to morph.

Mary, the conference leader, called me on the phone and said she'd been thinking and praying. She sensed God was telling her that something else needed to happen as a message to the churched women who would attend the conference. Mary used the metaphor of a party for what was typically happening in many churches and what just might be happening at the conference. "We're going to Chicago to throw a party for ourselves, and we're leaving Chicago out of it," she sighed. "It's not right. We're going to lock ourselves up in a hotel. But we need to go out onto the street."

I said we were there to serve. Our team typically performs the kinds of things I have written about elsewhere in this book: The Bible, true stories and prayers. What did she have in mind?

"Can your team do street theatre?" Mary asked.

I tried to be supportive. I said that we would do what we could to be missionaries to Chicago, but we did not know anything about street theatre. All our work had been rehearsed for the carefully controlled confines of worship settings. No, we could not do street theatre.

"That's okay," said Mary. "It doesn't have to be real street theatre. What I'd really like to try is to pray with the people of Chicago." The idea was still forming, so I kept listening. She explained that she had heard about prayer teams at a recent Billy Graham crusade in New York. People went out on the street and offered to pray for New Yorkers as they walked past. She heard that no one refused the offer for prayer. Her idea was that our team would do street theatre to attract people to stop and watch, and she would gather prayer teams to approach those who stopped.

I repeated that street theatre was a special set of skills which we did not have. She said she had an idea of someone in New York who could train our team, and so I agreed to schedule our team to be on call for the entire conference.

Several months went by. Members of our team passed through New York City twice, but no one emerged to teach us about street theatre. The conference was getting closer, and our team was getting more unsettled about what was being asked of us. Phone calls went back and forth with no certain plan.

One day, Mary called with a definite plan. She had found a street performer who had years of experience interviewing people on the street. The new plan was to have the street performer confront people as they walked past, and then if they would talk with her, she would eventually turn them over to us to enact a prayer for them. Individuals would also be standing by watching for those who might want a personal and more private prayer.

I tried to maintain a supportive posture, but I was seriously concerned. If we failed as street performers, how would this be Christian service to the people of Chicago? I have always said to my students that bad Christian drama is still bad drama. And would our failure on the street not be heard about around the conference, undercutting our credibility when it came time to perform the play that we were first invited to perform?

The conference director assured me that it was an experiment, and we could pull the plug anytime. Well...we knew how to pray enacted prayers, so we would be doing something we felt quite comfortable doing. I agreed. We would go forward, a step at a time.

On the first day of the conference, the street performer did not show up. Her flight from New York had been delayed. So we did an enacted prayer to support the prayer teams. It was beautiful. It reminded us that God was already out on the street. Individuals on the prayer teams went around the hotel lobby and onto the street out front and ended up praying for several people. A Bible study leader at the conference had a harp with her, and she played it on the street while my students chatted with the homeless people. It was a step forward, and we were eager for the next day's work.

Late that night, the street performer arrived and she was a ball of human energy. I could see right away why people would stop and talk with her. She was a person to whom it was almost impossible to say no. I felt this is what it must have been like to confront the Apostle Paul on the street.

And then the wrangling began. She liked the idea of enacted prayer, but she wanted us to act out prayers using people on the street to play themselves. I said no. She said yes. I said no. She said try. I said no. She asked why? I gave a bunch of reasons, including the fact that when people are performing in an enacted prayer, they cannot see what is going on, and so they miss the power of the image to carry with them. To say nothing of the fact that most people going by on the street are not performers and so they would feel uncomfortable, awkward, and might giggle their way through the prayer. We went to bed that night at a stalemate. The street performer agreed that we would pray the next day the way we had rehearsed, but she acknowledged that she was not giving up her position.

The next day arrived sunny and clear. We hauled the sound equipment onto the street. My team was ready to go. The street performer arrived wearing angel wings. She also had a blow-up green couch, video cameras, and signs saying that people were entering a film shoot. A film shoot? Sure enough, cameras would roll. I had no idea (and I still do not know) what would happen to this footage. But I had told Mary that we would step forward, so we did. While we were waiting for the street performer to set up, I saw someone I knew. I asked her if we could pray an enacted prayer for her. She said yes, and so we did. Immediately someone else nearby put up her hand and asked if we would pray for her daughter who was due to have a baby that very day. We prayed that prayer, too.

Then the street angel took over. Our interface was awkward at best. Her pattern was to ask people what they wanted in life. What was their ideal? What would make them happy? Then she would turn and look at me. That was our cue to enact a prayer giving them what they wanted. It sort of felt to me like prayer-as-slot-machine. We prayed a lot of prayers for good jobs which paid well. It was getting strange. Finally one man said that his ideal was to spend his life sitting on the couch with a money tree at his right hand and elves serving him. The street performer looked at me, and I shook my head—we would not be praying that prayer. Remember when I told you that you could not say no to her? She saw her opportunity, and she said to the man, "Play yourself in this prayer. Sit right here on my couch."

What followed can hardly be described. My students tried to be supportive without actually creating a prayer. They tried to simply show the man what he was asking for. They created a frozen image of the man's ideal. Their stools were stacked one upon the other to represent the man's money tree. The street angel herself represented the elves. Then it was over, and the street performer said, "Was that what you wanted?" The man said, "Yeah, but I didn't feel happy." I walked away. It was time to pack up.

I glanced to the side, and suddenly standing there grinning at me was one of my former students, Heidi. She was previously a member of our team. She graduated two years ago. Now she had come into Chicago because she had heard we would be here. And she had come to find us on the street. She hugged us all like long-lost friends, which we were. She helped us carry the gear back into the hotel.

That night we performed *Sioux Center Sudan*. It was nearly perfect. There were women there from all over the world, including Sioux Center and Sudan. Arlene was there. After the play, Karen got up and said, "I'd like you to meet the real Arlene Schuiteman." The women leapt to their feet in applause. It was the sort of moment that a playwright can only hope to see a few times this side of heaven. I had dramatized a story that Arlene had lived. And so many of these women in the room had prayed for her throughout her long career in Africa, sending her money, and letters and supplies. It was, for all of us, the culmination of a long journey.

The next day, we went back onto the street to pray, and

some friends of the money tree man stopped by. They told the street angel that they had a long conversation with their friend about what makes a life a happy life. And then they asked us to enact a prayer for one of them. After the prayer, the woman requesting the prayer said, "It feels good to be reminded that God is there with me." And they walked away.

There was a bit of hope at its conclusion, but I was glad when our prayer experiment was over. The street angel and I parted as friends. One lady from the conference even said that praying on the street was her favorite part of the whole conference.

But a personal struggle had arisen in me. I had a nagging feeling that a chasm was opening in me, an awareness of a blank spot in my life—something out of whack in some way. I traced it back to a moment on the street when the street angel had asked a young couple point blank if they believed in God. If I were to turn my internal anxiety into a tiny skit, it might go something like this:

STREET ANGEL
Do you two believe in God?

JEFF'S INNER VOICE
You have no idea what you're doing. What if they say they don't?! What will you say? Do you have a plan?

MAN
No, I don't believe in God.

JEFF'S INNER VOICE
See! See what I mean. You can't just accost people on the street about matters of faith. You're just going to create hostility.

STREET ANGEL

Why not?

JEFF'S INNER VOICE

No, no, no. Don't go there. People don't want to talk
about religion in a public way.

MAN

I just don't. I take responsibility for my own life.

STREET ANGEL
(turning to the woman)
How about you? Do you believe in God?

JEFF'S INNER VOICE

Whoa. Of course she doesn't! She's with him.

WOMAN

Sometimes.

MAN

You do?

WOMAN

Yes, I do. I want to anyway. I want it to be true that
God is there for me.

MAN

We'd better get going. Nice talking to you.

STREET ANGEL

You, too.

JEFF'S INNER VOICE
What just happened?

I knew that the street angel was not what you might call a mature Christian. But I was seeing that she loved people, and she was willing to open the door of her heart and invite them in, whoever and however they were, whether they were ready or not and whether she was ready or not. It was weird, and messy and just plain hard work. But it was starting to feel like the story behind the Acts of the Apostles. Much of my Christian life these days has to do with what happens inside the church and its worship, and that place tends to be about stories that are complete. What about the incomplete stories—stories that will be stories someday but are not yet?

What is my real relationship to story—am I willing not only to tell stories but to live in one? Not always to know the end? To have faith like Arlene and Vandy, believing God not for what he does but for who he is? Am I willing to be an Abraham—to follow God even when he has not told me where we are going?

I think God knew I was struggling, so he spoke through Heidi to affirm that everything about story—story making and storytelling—are his domain. Heidi had stayed overnight with one of the women on our team, and she and I ended up carrying bottles of water across the hotel lobby. We were taking them to give away on the street. "Here," she said, "Stack them in my arms like firewood." I did, and as we slowly walked, Heidi's arms round and full, she said, "People forget things easily, including who God is, that God is. He knows this about us, so he creates memory-markers. Ebenezers. That's what stories are. Big stones for remembering God. In fact, I think that's why God makes things happen in our lives. So they can be turned into stories about him."

On the final night of the conference, I was walking with Karen along the river next to the hotel. We came upon an ancient, saintly woman who had been at the conference and saw the play that our team performed. She said, "Jeff, we need to tell the stories of God's work." I said, "Yes. If they're not told, they'll be lost." She just stared at me, and then she flung her arms around my neck.

Authenticity

Church is too slick, too good, too polished to be real. And the twenty-something hunger for raw authenticity . . .
— Mike Sares
Out of Ur *blog, August 21, 2006*

O nce there was a couple traveling in Hawaii," said our pastor at the start of worship one Sunday. At our church we
recognize this moment as the beginning of a worship journey
that is shaped, in part, by story. Sometimes the "Once there was
. . ." is the start to a story that will be told completely in the first
couple of minutes. And sometimes it is the beginning of a story
that will resurface several times in the worship service and will
be completed near the end of the service.

I will return to the story about the couple traveling in
Hawaii. But first, let me give you an example of the way such a
beginning to a service might work its way through an entire
worship structure. Here is a very simple service-length story that
we used at our church a couple of years ago.

Once there was a man riding in a chariot,

said one of the worship leaders at the beginning of the service,

*and we will travel with him today as he encounters a
Book, a Person, and some Water. Let's pray as we begin
our journey.*

During this service, there were several mini-testimonies in
which the congregation was given contemporary images of each
of the three elements (Book, Person, Water) without a lot of ex-
planation. I was part of the platform team that day, and I recall
I started the "Book" section as follows:

A Book.

I held up a leather-bound volume; it was obviously a Bible, without needing to state it.

*This was given to me as a present when I graduated from
college. The binding fell apart a few years ago, but I
didn't want to let it go yet, so I put it back together with
hot glue. It says inside, "To Jeff from Karen, May, 1976."*

Two more people told about a Bible of theirs—not a full story,
just a quick verbal snapshot.

Several mini-testimonies or images were shared, in associ-
ation with personal Bibles, personal encounters with Jesus, and
personal experiences with baptism. They were an average of
thirty seconds each. For the second one, I said:

*A Person.
I was thirteen years old. I had just come back from a
week at summer camp. It was late at night, and I was in
my bed in the dark, crying. I was crying because I had
just understood, for the first time in my life, the truth
that Jesus had suffered terribly, and it was for me—it*

was because of my sinfulness. And that night, crying into my pillow, I said, "Jesus, I'm sorry. Thank you. I believe in you. You are my Lord. Forever."

Songs, prayers, screen images, gestures, and other service elements continued between the tiny stories. When it was time for the third one, I said:

Some water.
It was on this platform. Earlier, a teenage girl had asked if she could be baptized by pouring, since it was possibly the way Jesus was baptized. The pastor had said yes, so the girl's father put some plastic down and covered that with several layers of towels and then two large swaths of fabric, one white piece to cover the towels, and one blue piece to symbolize the river Jordan.
The girl wore a simple gown, and she knelt in her bare feet. Her pastor said, "I baptize you in the name of the Father, and Son and Holy Spirit." And he gently poured an entire pitcher of water over the girl's head and shoulders as she wept.

Most of the congregation knew I was speaking of my own daughter's baptism a couple of years before. Then just before the sermon, a young man—a college student—stood up and said,

Once upon a time there was a man riding in a chariot. And he encountered a Book, a Person and some Water. Remember these words as recorded in the Book that we love.

And then the young man spoke from memory Acts 8:26–39. You will remember this to be the story of the Ethiopian eunuch reading from scripture as he rode along, with Philip running to catch him and helping him discover Jesus in the Hebrew prophecy—ending with Philip baptizing this new believer into discipleship.

The remainder of the service was the sermon, based on the text from Acts, followed by communion. They each held images and music which connected our hearts and minds back to themes introduced earlier in the worship hour.

I have just given you an example of a simple service structure (Book, Person, Water) that grows in complexity by connection to many stories. The larger story hovers over the entire service, with many smaller stories inside that one big story.

I would like to return now to our pastor's story of the couple traveling in Hawaii. Initially, I thought the story was not an example of a service-length story. I thought it was a story completely told in less than two minutes. But I was wrong, sort of, as you will see.

Once there was a couple traveling in Hawaii.

Our pastor continued,

This couple believed that God somehow led them to get on a particular tour bus. They followed this leading even though they didn't know why. (Was it a direct word like the kind that the prophets talk of, or was it a simple inner prompting that one of them received? We don't know.) All we know is that they understood that God was leading, and they were following.

On the bus, they got into a conversation with a man seated in front of them, and soon they were all talking about God and faith. The couple came to believe that this is why God wanted them on the bus. While they traveled from stop to stop, they continued their conversation. The man seemed interested, but he wasn't a Christian when they started, and, as far as anyone could tell, he wasn't a Christian when they said goodbye to one another. It seemed that when the tour was over the couple could only trust that God was doing something, but they still didn't know what it was.

What that couple didn't know was that there was a man sitting behind them eavesdropping. He was a man who was in a desperate struggle with God and faith. The man had prayed, saying to God that if he was real would he please reveal the answers to each of several specific questions that were standing between him and a commitment to faith. On the bus that day, he sat behind this couple. He heard them speak to the man in front of them, answering each of the questions he had asked God about. And when he got off the bus that day, he had the answer to his prayer, and he placed his trust in God.

After our pastor finished this story, he asked us to bow our heads for prayer.

The story had reminded me of the chariot ride with Philip and the Ethiopian. But as our pastor prayed the opening prayer, I also thought of a student in my Drama and Worship class who told a story that seemed too good to be true. I asked her what her source was and she said, "It was sent to me in an email." I asked her if it was a real event, and she said, "I think so." I asked her if she knew who it happened to, and she admitted she did not. It was one of those internet stories that circulate as fact but remain unverifiable. There in church that morning, I felt as if our pastor was attempting to inspire our worship by perpetrating an urban myth, and I felt manipulated.

After the amen to the prayer, our pastor said something

that made me deeply grateful:

> *The man seated behind that couple on the bus is a member of our church. His name is Jamie. He told that story in last Sunday night's service, and I thought you would all want to hear it, so I repeated it today. Jamie is here this morning and after the service, you can ask him to give you more of the details.*

I do not necessarily advocate teasing your audience by withholding information, but I do celebrate the ultimate power of this story. Much of its power is due to its authenticity.

As the service continued, my sense of celebration grew. Our pastors were preaching a series on the favorite Bible passages of members of their congregation. This particular Sunday, a woman of the congregation stepped to the pulpit to share one of her favorite passages: Psalm 62. She said, "I brought my Bible up here, but this Psalm is hidden in my heart." She looked us in the eye, and she spoke the entire Psalm from memory, slowly and joyfully. It was a breathtaking moment. Then she said,

> *I trust God. For example, I'm trusting him right now concerning taking in two children. A six-year-old and a three-year-old are in an emergency situation, and their care has been offered to Dan and me. This was easy for me to answer, but now we are waiting for the next step. We are trusting God, and we invite you to pray with us.*

Before she could return to her seat, one of our pastors stepped up next to her, and said, "Let's pray right now."

I have been reporting to you authentic stories of trust from the Sunday morning worship service at my home church on August 27, 2006, in Orange City, Iowa.

Every story told in worship must be authentic. By saying "authentic", I mean that the hearers must be able to trust the details. In the case of real events, you must provide enough facts, even if it requires the vulnerability which is necessary to verify personal facts. We will accept both actual event stories and fictional stories. But it is usually pretty important for us to know which of those two you are telling. In other words, if it is not an actual event, you should somehow communicate, "Once upon a time. . . ." and then we will know what you are up to. We tend to lose trust when you resist the vulnerability necessary for verification or if you try to present a piece of fiction as a piece of history.

Those who lose trust in you can also, whether fair or not, lose trust in your message.

More Like a Novel Than a Magazine

In the main, Christians do not have an abstract, philosophical concept of God; rather, they understand God primarily through the stories in the Bible....

— Thomas Long
Testimony

On a beautiful fall morning in my town, I went over to a local church that was hosting a worship workshop. I was only able to stay for awhile because I also wanted to attend the Festival of New Music at our college.

At the worship workshop, Howard Vanderwell from the Calvin Institute of Christian Worship was talking about the relationship of theme and worship. He said, "Worship has a beginning, a central portion, and an end." Ah ha—story structure—I said to myself. Norma de Waal Malefyt, his colleague, added, "If you want an image for the thematic shape of worship, think of worship more like a novel than a magazine." There it is again, simple and sweet. Then I slipped out the door to the college.

At the college, the concert was already in progress. I picked up a program, concentrated on the music, and took the program home with me. Standing in my kitchen, I read that one piece of vocal music had been based entirely on brief stories. The composer wrote that he prefers working from prose rather than poetry. He uses stories gleaned from many sources. Reading through the stories, it seemed immediately clear to me that someone had pared the stories down to their bare essential actions. They have "a beginning, a central portion, and an end"— little else. Here is one of the stories, taken directly from the program that I picked up at the concert:

> *Osip Mandelshtam, Russia's great poet, wrote a poem, privately circulated, critical of Stalin. He was sentenced to forced labor. He died as a result, and his widow was forced to travel from one province to another, till her shoes got so worn they barely hung to her feet. She found a cobbler in one small city where she was hiding. She told him the story of her love, her fear, and her sorrow. He looked at her and said, "You'll never go without shoes again."*

Standing there in my kitchen, I started singing, "Lord, I want to be a Christian in my heart." Then the worship leader in me imagined that sequence in a worship service: someone tells that story of Osip's wife, and then we sing that song, "Lord I want to be. . . ." There is no more comment than that. The sequence makes us ask, "Who is the Christian in that story? Is it Osip? His wife? The cobbler?" We do not have to be told the answer. In fact, the story's evocation of the question helps us apply the song to our own experience and our own longing toward Christlikeness. Something inside us makes us say, "Yes, Lord, count me in!" in a way that is deeper and more long-lasting than singing the song by itself. This linking takes us one step toward the structure that Howard and Norma were talking about.

If the above sequence of a story followed by a worship song is simply dropped into a worship service, we still have "magazine worship." But if it is dropped into a service in which the scripture text is Jesus sending his disciples from town to town, taking nothing with them, then we are getting closer to Norma's image of "novel worship." It all gets connected together, but in an evocative rather than explicit manner.

A story by itself is still good. A song by itself is still good. A scripture by itself is still good. But if a worship planner can choose to include a little story in support of a larger story that connects to *the* story, might that not be a beautiful thing?

The Differing Tasks of Text and Speech

O, it
offends me to the soul to hear a robustious periwig-pated fellow
tear a passion to tatters, to very rags, to split the ears of the
groundlings, who for the most part are capable of nothing but
inexplicable dumbshows and noise: I would have such a fellow
whipped for o'erdoing Termagant; it out-herods Herod: pray
you, avoid it.

— *Hamlet*, ACT 3, SCENE 2

The professor of systematic theology was preaching during Friday morning chapel at the seminary. I have also heard her preach in the chapel at our college in Iowa. My experience is she reads her well-crafted sermons. She reads at a consistent, slow pace. I love to hear her preach, but sometimes she disappears into those pages, with her face and voice turned downward. I confess that I occasionally want to interrupt her and say, "Just wanted to let you know we're still here."

But today at the seminary, something different happened at one moment in her delivery. Her text was a story from Luke's gospel. Jesus goes to the synagogue on the Sabbath, and he is teaching. A possessed man has come there that day. A demon cries out through the man.

What do you want with us, Jesus of Nazareth?
Have you come to destroy us?

The professor of systematic theology told us perhaps the demon voices all of humanity's cry to its redeemer.

What do you want with us, Jesus of Nazareth?
Have you come to destroy us?

This questioning became a refrain within her sermon, and she read it several times.

And then she looked up suddenly from her notes. She looked us in the eye. And this time she spoke from memory.

What do you want with us, Jesus of Nazareth?
Have you come to destroy us?

She did not cry out. Her voice was calm and quiet. It sent shivers down my spine. The words themselves were so powerful. Understatement was just the right tool for the moment.

The story sets it up—it is Sabbath at a synagogue. Jesus is present. And an evil spirit enters the room. Jesus begins teaching, but the evil spirit interrupts with its own sad agenda.

And because of her level gaze, I got her point. The evil spirit is me.

A gentle reminder was perfect. My eardrums did not need to be split to open the door of my heart.

Two other examples of this gentle technique come quickly to mind. In Jeffrey Sweet's play *Bluff*, there is a character who is narrating his own actions. He says, "A scream," and the implication is that, within the story, he has just screamed. He does not need to scream the words. The words carry their own weight in this circumstance. A calm, quiet voice seems especially suited to the moment.

The other moment I am remembering is a discovery I made in my own performance of a play with Karen recently. I was playing the role of the Fisherman in the classic story of *The Fisherman and His Wife*. (Our dramatization of that story is in the APPENDICES.) In the final moments of this little play, the Fisherman encounters the Fish for the last time. The story asks us to imagine the wind howling, and I was used to playing the scene with a loud voice to be heard over that imaginary weather. But this time through, I remembered that the Fish is enchanted and does not need me to yell in order to hear me. "Perhaps," I thought to myself, "the emotional weight of the scene would be more poignant if it were played quietly. The Fisherman's heart is breaking, and he can barely speak." I tried it in rehearsal, and this choice allowed Karen, playing the Fish, to speak her lines quietly as well. She said,

> *No, Fisherman.*
> *There is only one maker of the sunrise.*
> *Go home, Fisherman. Go home.*

Their quiet exchange suggested a shared embrace of the truth in the Fish's words, and it also suggested that the storm was over. Karen and I decided to change our performance of that scene. I cannot be positive, but my guess is that the quiet choice was much more evocative for the audience.

On the day that the professor of systematic theology told the story of the synagogue demon, I traveled into Chicago to see a play. It was a new version of *Peter Pan*, with all the dark edges of the original Barrie story brought into sharper focus. It was no longer a children's play. It was an attempt to construct a complex tale that spoke to us adults about our psychological relationship with the child selves that we had, ostensibly, tried to leave behind. It was certainly an interesting project with great potential. The talented acting ensemble spoke and moved with great energy. Apparently, they had also been instructed to speak with great volume, even though it was a very small theatre. A few of the characters, especially that leader of the lost boys, Peter Pan, and the evil Captain Hook, screamed the entire play. I am guessing that they thought it supported their script's theme concerning the dangerous landscape of the human mind. I got the idea, but I was worn out and unmoved. They had indeed split our eardrums but nevertheless failed to open the doors of our hearts.

Matching interpretation to meaning does not always dictate that voice and words do the same thing. It sometimes means just the opposite.

The Body Is a Storyteller

Nope.

— John Pfautz

(This is what John answered me when I asked him if his friends in Africa would think they had worshiped if they had gone to church and there was no dancing.)

Kristi is one of the college students on our worship planning team at church. One day she stopped by my office at the college. She looked up at the large sheets of laminated white poster board stuck on my wall. One of them is labeled "Ideas." One idea listed there is "Dance—Amanda—ballet." Some of us on the worship planning team have seen Amanda present liturgical ballet in chapel. And we have worked with her around the theatre department. Our hope has been to woo her to our church for a Sunday.

Kristi asked, "Can we have tap dance some Sunday?" I hesitated long enough to wonder what tap and worship have to do with one another. The answer came in a heartbeat: what they have in common is a mood of celebration. Within two seconds, I said, "Absolutely. Write it on the board." One of us grabbed the marker and wrote, "Tap dance."

I did not know how to accomplish such a thing. We have a 1970s shag rug all over our sanctuary. And how would tap dancing fit into the flow of corporate worship? Nevertheless, I wanted to encourage my team to dream big, so the words stayed on the wall.

The details followed. Yesterday, we had tap dance at worship. In this case, I do not think I asked for our pastor's approval. The worship planning team was all on board, so I was not being a lone ranger, but it was just weird enough that I decided not to cause the pastor to lose any sleep over it. I wanted him to be able to blame me completely. I have earned some chips over the years, so I decided to risk a few on this one. I was taking a risk with the pastor and a risk with the congregation. Risk-taking within public worship is possible in a context of trust, vision, love and prayer (lots of prayer). It is also helped by storytelling and series preaching. Leaders in this environment carry with them a sense of humor that accepts fallibility, not cultivating sloppiness, but recognizing that worship does not always need to be perfect—sometimes we will fail. It is amazing what a congregation will accept when high school or college students are involved.

I told the church janitor that I would be bringing in a four by eight platform on Saturday. We borrowed the platform from the theatre shop, where the dancers practiced on it earlier in the week.

Kristi worked with Megan, another student worship planner, to craft a service that bounced between celebration and lament, never letting us focus exclusively on ourselves or even on the stuff of our gratitude. We were saying "Thank you," but we kept shifting focus. How can I describe this shifting? I wish you had been there. The methodology was to let the pendulum swing. So we had celebration and lament, joy and sorrow, sweet and sour, raucous and quiet. We never focused on the gift alone, but we kept returning to the Giver. Megan chose songs that actually referred to this pendulum swing, starting with Matt Redman's "Blessed Be the Name." But we did not start with the song's usual initial lyrics. This service started with a single voice singing, "You give and take away, You give and take away."

A bit later in the service, we were all on our feet, singing with passion. Kristi was singing with other members of the team just upstage of the low platform we had brought in.

> *Open up the doors and let the music play*
> *Let the streets resound with singing*
> *Songs that bring your hope*
> *Songs that bring your joy*
> *Dancers who dance upon injustice*

While we sang along with the two drummers, two guitarists, and two violinists, Kristi was on the platform in one step and tapping in the next. It was a simple and subtle addition to the joy in the room without any distraction or undue attention drawn. My guess is that some people present did not even notice yet.

It was just the set up.

After the offering, there came an integrated eight minute segment of worship. Here is how it went. First, we sang together one stanza and one refrain of the hymn "How Great Thou Art." By the end of the song, a beloved lady from our congregation was standing on the platform. (I mentioned in an earlier chapter that good stories bear repeating, and such repetition cements relationships. Here comes the full version of a story hinted at previously.)

> *My name is Marietta Vandersall. I'm sixty-six years old,*
> *and I'm a retired secretary.*
> *Come with me on a journey. Our family had moved*

to Orange City in August. It was now November. I began having pains in my stomach, so I go to the doctor. He tells me I have a stone in my gall bladder. In the process of running the blood test he discovers that I have kidney disease. He refers me to a specialist in Sioux City, where I am told that within a year I will either need a kidney transplant or be on dialysis. It was a shock but not totally unexpected. My mother, aunt, and uncle had all died from kidney failure. We knew we had to tell the children who were 11, 15, and 16. So we have a family conference. I try to tell them in a positive way that everything will be alright. I don't want any pessimists—God is in control.

Two years went by, and I was living a very normal life—going to all the usual school and church activities and working full-time. Each time I go to the doctor he is surprised and tells me he knows my kidneys will fail soon and I will have to go on dialysis. All I can think each time is of the song "How Great Thou Art." He will allow me see my children grow up.

In August the doctor tells me that I have to go on the list for a transplant but that it could take up to two years to receive a kidney. I continue to function. Then in October my blood counts begin showing a decreased kidney function. They make plans to put me on dialysis. It is Thursday. I am scheduled to begin dialysis, but when I go to the doctor I have a bad cold. He says to come back the following Tuesday.

Tuesday, October 11, 1983. At 3:00 A.M. the telephone rings. I answer it thinking something must be wrong in our family. It's the Transplant Office in Iowa City. "We have a kidney that we think is a good match for you," they say. "We need you to be in Iowa City by noon."

Again, the song "How Great Thou Art" is ringing in

my heart. My husband and I begin making preparations for the five hour trip to Iowa City. After getting the three children up and helping them know what they have to do while I am gone, I go to the office to clear my desk and prepare for someone to take my place. We make phone calls to family members and friends asking them to pray. By 6:00 A.M. we are on the road—just my husband and me.

After arriving at the hospital, they do more tests and determine that the kidney is indeed a very good match for me. The surgery takes place at 5:00 P.M. that day. While still on the operating table the kidney begins to function. "My God How Great Thou Art." By midnight that night I am fully awake and welcoming my sister and her husband from Kansas City into the hospital room.

I spend thirty days in the hospital (and a total of sixty days out of the next four months). I go through three rejections. I have pneumonia. I get the CMV virus and various other side effects from the medication. But I can only celebrate the grace of God and sing "How Great Thou Art."

Without saying anything to other people about how that particular song had gotten me through the journey, the very first Sunday I was back here in church, what song did we sing? "How Great Thou Art."

It's now twenty-two years later, and my kidney is functioning as well or better than most people my age.

At this point, one of the instruments picks up the song again, but we're not going to sing yet. We just need that melody and a rhythm. As Marietta steps off the platform, Megan steps into her place and begins to say, from memory the words we all know so well:

The Lord is my shepherd; I shall not want.
He maketh me to lie down in green pastures:
he leadeth me beside the still waters.

Who had the idea for what happened next? I do not know. I just know that it was breathtaking. Somewhere around,

Yea, though I walk through the valley of the shadow of
death, I will fear no evil . . .

Kristi is on that platform, feet beginning to make sound with the scripture. She is tap dancing to Psalm 23! And for some reason it makes sense.

Thou anointest my head with oil; my cup runneth over.

Tap, tap, tap! Story, scripture, song, sound and movement lift our hearts to the Lord. Megan finishes the Psalm and suddenly we are on our feet singing Marietta's favorite song. And as we sing, Lois is beside Kristi and they are tap dancing in unison, fast and hard, and it is perfect.

After the service, I am the last one in the sanctuary, picking up. Diane, whose husband has just been diagnosed with liver cancer, comes rushing back up the stairs. "I was outside starting to dance," she says, "and I realized I should come back to say thank you." (I forgot to tell you, the sermon that day was about Jesus and the ten lepers.) Diane hugs me, asks me to pass it along to the team and skips back out the door.

To Speak with Understanding

Moreover, it will be thus appreciated of what benefit and con-
solation the pope and those that belong to him have deprived
the Church; for he has reduced the psalms, which ought to be
true spiritual songs, to a murmuring among themselves with-
out any understanding.

— John Calvin

While spending a couple of weeks at the Calvin Institute of Christian Worship, I walked down to John Witvliet's office one day to ask him the question, "When did congregations start reading aloud together? What's the history of that worship practice?" I thought if anyone would know the answer, it would be John. He did not. He did point me to some research options. I was especially fascinated by *The Worship of the English Puritans* by Horton Davies, but it was not definitive on the subject of unison readings.

Leaf through worship history. Worship of the God of Abraham, Isaac, and Jacob happened in oral cultures, not generally literate cultures. This continued from the ancient Israelites all the way past the apostles. No one was getting a bulletin at the door, bringing their personal scriptures to church, or pulling prayer books out of the pew rack. When did that happen? When Thomas Cranmer gathered together the Book of Common Prayer in the middle of the 1500s, were there enough copies printed so that every worshiper could see a copy? Surely not yet. They had to spend some time fighting over whether or not that book was to be an official document of this new Protestant expression of faith, or even if there would be such a new expression. Then there is the question of whether enough adult worshipers could read to make it worthwhile to attempt a group reading? I am guessing that a few generations went by with memorized portions of such liturgical devices as the Eucharistic litany being the only unison speech heard in worship. No readings in the typical church. Not yet. Maybe the 1600s. Maybe not until much later.

My point in tracking down the history behind this practice is to discover what need was being addressed by unison readings? What value was being achieved?

I am on this quest because it seems to me that something essential has been lost.

I grew up in a church that read what we called "responsive readings." They were in the back of the hymnal. They were verses of scripture from various places in the Bible, gathered on a specific theme. So you might find a group of verses on sin or grace or hope. I sometimes wondered where these passages were, and then I saw the teeny-tiny references all grouped at the bottom, and I would spend half of the sermon looking up the passages and reading the original context. I was old enough to have grown wary of proof-texting even though I did not yet know the term.

Then I went away to college and learned about Catholic missals, and the Book of Common Prayer, and that a responsive reading from the back of my boyhood hymnal could sometimes be called a "litany" depending upon how the passage was organized. The impression I had was that this practice was as old as

Moses and as common as singing and prayer.

But I had a problem. When I finished reading, I had no idea what I had just read. My focus was on making sure I did not mispronounce words or read the leader's part by mistake and make a fool of myself by speaking solo. I tried not to go too fast or too slow, and I tried to figure out where this particular congregation was used to putting the pauses. I was murmuring without any understanding.

I tried to solve my problem by looking ahead in the worship service. If I had time, I did a little private practicing in my pew before the service. To get the meaning, I resorted to my childhood practice of going back over the text during the sermon.

These tactics helped a little bit, but they did not solve the additional problem that this group of believers did not sound as if we believed. Even if there was understanding, which was often in question, we were still murmuring. As I listened to myself and those around me, it seemed as if we were concerned more with unison speech than with meaningful speech. Our voices were hollow—more sound than truth. We were proof that the phrase, "He gave us a litany of reasons," can be taken to mean, "He gave us a bunch of words, but they were inconclusive."

One day I had an opportunity to try and address the problem. I was attending the Free Methodist church in New Brighton, Pennsylvania, and the Sunday School director asked me to take the opening five minutes of the adult Sunday School. This was just a gathering time in the main sanctuary before everyone went to their classes. It was a few minutes that could be used for announcements or a song or a story. It was a chance for us to see who was there, to say good morning, to help visitors find a Sunday School class, and generally to cheer each other on for the work of the morning. Anything that happened from the front of the room was really up to the Sunday School director. She was busy that day, so she asked me to cover for her. I was not any sort of official worship leader at that church, but I had looked ahead at the worship service that would follow Sunday School. I saw there was a responsive reading of a Psalm printed in the bulletin. I seized the moment. I said, "Good morning. Get out your bulletins." I asked them to read the Psalm aloud with me. We did it. And then I talked them into proclaiming the scripture instead of just reading it.

In other words, I asked them to rehearse.

In the available five minutes, we looked at individual sections of the Psalm and talked about the images and sounds that were implied in the text. It is now many years ago, but I believe it was Psalm 100 (NRSV). Verse one belonged to the leader.

Make a joyful noise to the LORD, all the earth.

I urged them to take the leader's encouragement seriously and to be *loud*. It took us three tries as we practiced, but we got there, and I could see that the people were delighted with the way we planned to proclaim verse two the way the Psalmist was urging us.

Worship the LORD with gladness;
Come into his presence with singing.

But our rehearsal was not finished. We noticed that our next section had repetition.

It is he that made us, and we are his;
We are his people, and the sheep of his pasture.

Usually when there is repetition, you do not say the repeated phrase the same both times. The repetition is there for emphasis, so you try to slow down and capture that emphasis. We practiced a pause after "It is he that made us, and we are his." (Pause.) And then we practiced extra slowness and building emphasis throughout the next line. *We / are / his / people! / / / And the sheep of his pasture!* We were quieter than the opening shout, but we spoke with surety and energy.

The leader's next verse had images of city walls and crowds of people performing worship with rehearsed spectacle.

> *Enter his gates with thanksgiving,*
> *and his courts with praise.*

This verse is about the city of God! It is a processional! It is a special moment! It is about a people whose gratefulness is evident for all to see right away. This verse is no place for dour droning. It is about a celebration, and it sounds like it. Our next verse rose to the occasion, calling all within earshot to join us!

> *Give thanks to him,*
> *bless his name.*

We topped our first noisy verse with a huge parade-like sound of the blasting trumpets and clashing cymbals borrowed from Psalm 150!

As we ended, our voices became slow, quiet and sure—a sound for the ages:

> *. . . his steadfast love endures forever,*
> *and his faithfulness to all generations.*

After Sunday School, I warned the pastor that when he led the Psalm, he should not be too surprised if the congregation sounded as if they meant it.

They came through. It was a true spiritual song, spoken without murmuring and with great understanding.

It is very rare that you have an opportunity to rehearse a congregation in reading aloud together. If you have the opportunity, seize it. If you do not, there are still other ways to make a difference. The script can have in parentheses simple coaching words like, "Shouted!" or, "With great joy," or even, "Slowly, but with energy." In addition, the pace, energy and emotion of the leader can provide cues to the congregation. If the leader simply pauses before plowing ahead to their own next line, it can slow us all down enough to realize that something is happening other than a unison race to the last punctuation mark.

I doubt the time has come to stop reading aloud together. But until I discover why we started it in the first place, I remain uncertain. Many congregations are now quite dependent upon reading aloud together, and it would be unwise for worship leaders in those situations suddenly to disband the practice. I am guessing there are worship leaders who have found creative ways to bless their congregations with restorative work in this area. I hope they will teach the rest of us.

Of Art and Relationship

When I was a kid, I went to church with my mother, and the minister would speak to my mother, "How're you, Miz Craddock?" and the five of us kids would go along like little ducks after our mother. "How're you, sonny? How're you, honey? How're you, sonny? How're you, honey?"

But I remember when another minister came to our church, and about his fifth or sixth Sunday when I went along there, he said, "Fred, how're you doing?" He was the best minister that ever was at that church, because there's a big difference between "sonny" and "Fred."

— Fred Craddock
Craddock Stories

My phone rang, and it was a man named Leon. He was from out of state, but he was in a nearby town visiting a friend. Some mutual acquaintances had suggested to him that he might want to talk with me. Did I have a few minutes to talk and could he come and see me? Come ahead, I told him.

He arrived at my office in the DeWitt Theatre Arts Center twenty minutes later. Leon knew the reputation of our college's theatre program. In fact, said Leon, he had attended our college and even acted in some plays here, long before my time. That was back when he did not really know what he wanted to do in life or even how he wanted to live.

Leon was eager to share his story, and my ears perk up whenever someone says, "I remember...," so I listened as he told me how he nearly flunked out of Northwestern, investigated another college, and, ultimately, left college behind, as well as his childhood faith. Years went by. He fell in love. He grew up. He finished college. He returned to faith. In fact, he became a preacher and pastor.

Eventually Leon told me the real reason he had come to see me. He wanted to become a performer of Bible stories. Red flags went up immediately, for the simple reason that Leon had a voice that reached out and vibrated in your chest. It was an ancient Greek theatre voice that grabs you by the throat and makes you sit up and listen. If Jesus had a voice like Leon's, it would not have been supernatural that his sermons and stories could be heard by thousands without electronic amplification. There is a subtle aesthetic temptation for a storyteller with a voice like Leon's to turn all that vocal power into melodrama. Storytelling invites an authentic relationship rather than glorification of vocal skill. A storyteller lives inside the story and invites the listener to travel along through the events. The great resonating voices typical of a pre-amplification style of performer can work well for storytelling (John Gielgud comes to mind), but such voices require training lest they sound a bit like organs with all the stops pulled out. Without nuance, such a voice overwhelms a story, becoming a cliché rather than an aid to honest communication. Well-meaning friends can say, "What a voice you have!" and thereby make matters even worse by causing the performer to measure success by the creation of a certain type of sound as opposed to attending to the relationship between performer and listener.

Leon went on to tell me of his fledgling steps in pursuit of his dream. He had memorized and presented the letters to Timothy, wearing a robe to represent Saint Paul. His next goal was triggered one day when Leon was at a gathering of Christian businessmen. The speaker had done something fairly simple. He had read to his audience Jesus's last words as published in the book of Acts:

> ... and you will be my witnesses in Jerusalem, and in all Judea and Samaria, and to the ends of the earth.
>
> (1:8b)

The speaker had asked, "Gentlemen, are you doing everything you can to fulfill Christ's great commission?" That question settled deep within Leon. As he described his feelings, I could tell he was carrying a true and lifelong passion. And one of the ways he was working out that passion was his plan to memorize and speak the entire book of Acts.

What suggestions, he asked, did I have for him? Then he glanced down at his watch and he said, "Oh, where has the time flown, I've got to go in a couple of minutes. But I want to hear what you have to say. Go ahead."

Two minutes. Two minutes?!

The truth of the matter is that art takes time, lots and lots of time, but the church (indeed, the culture at large) has been known to seek an easy tool and a quick product. The assumption is that artists are creative and can make much out of little. We artists ourselves fall prey to the rush of pride we feel when we seem to create something out of nothing. So, we fall into a pattern which nearly kills us. And who can resist such martyr-like activity when, like Leon, we come to believe that eternal souls hang in the balance and Jesus may return any minute.

Leon glanced again at his watch. I glanced at my watch, too. How could I compress four years of college into two minutes? Well, the truth is Leon will never take four more years of college. It is unlikely he will take even one acting class. The truth is what I had to say in these next two minutes might have to suffice. What would it be? I thought maybe I should change the subject and wish him well. Or maybe I could take a risk that, with very little relationship, I could become his teacher and he my student.

Maybe I only have you for two more minutes. I will tell you what I told Leon. I told him two things. I suggested that he wear his normal clothes. And I suggested that he look at the congregation when he talked.

It went something like this. "Leon, in two minutes . . . well, I don't really know you, but limited to two minutes, here are the two things I would like you to consider. Just try them out and see how they work. First, don't worry so much about Bible costumes. Wear what you have on in your everyday life. In fact, wear your own personality. You don't have to pretend to be somebody else. But you do have to let us see how these words that you are speaking are impacting you. They have to matter to you if you want them to matter to us. Tell these stories as if they changed your life and you cannot help but share them.

"Second, turn toward us when you speak. We're here in the room with you. Look us in the eye and talk to us. My sense is that we have to matter to the storyteller before the story will matter to us. Even if you're representing an historical person speaking to another historical person, put that unseen person out in front of you, not next to you on stage. In this way, we can see you, and it is more intimate than if you put the imaginary person on the stage. It is not about creating a reality on stage, but rather about evoking a reality within our imaginations."

He asked me to say a prayer for him. I was glad to pray for his future work in communicating the scriptures. And then he left. I do not know what Leon (or you) will do with my two suggestions, but I think they are a good place to start. They are basically about taking advantage of the performer's passion and the audience's imagination. As for the rest of my advice, that would take a relationship. And time.

Culture Stories

*Christian worship relates dynamically to culture in at least four ways. First, it is **transcultural**, the same substance for everyone everywhere, beyond culture. Second, it is **contextual**, varying according to the local situation (both nature and culture). Third, it is **counter-cultural**, challenging what is contrary to the Gospel in a given culture. Fourth, it is **cross-cultural**, making possible sharing between different local cultures. In all four dynamics, there are helpful principles which can be identified.*
   — 1996 statement of the Lutheran World Federation
   Study Team on Worship and Culture, Nairobi, Kenya

Since I lead worship mostly within intentionally informal congregations, I gain balance by learning from historical liturgical guides, some of which are mentioned in this book. For example, I have been greatly encouraged by the beauty and simplicity of the Nairobi Statement on culture and worship.

My teenaged daughter loves to tell me about worship experiences she has had when visiting relatives or on youth group trips. Here are portions of several of our conversations. I have filed them under the four points of the Nairobi Statement.

TRANSCULTURAL

JEFF

Did anything happen there that you would say happens in any Christian church anywhere anytime?

HANNAH

Most Christian churches sing, and they did lots of singing. But they didn't give us the words. I didn't know any of the songs, but it was still fun because everyone got so into it. At Aunt Kathy and Uncle Ken's church, I only knew one of the songs. I think it was a hymn. But the whole time people were singing their hearts out or lifting up their hands.

JEFF

Did they have communion at the big church in Omaha?

HANNAH

Yes. They all went to the front. Our group didn't go. There were long lines, and it took a long time.
(Pause.)
What do we do here when there's going to be a funeral? We just say someone died. People at the Minneapolis church mournfully celebrate it. They say, "We're going to celebrate the home-going of John Pearson on Saturday." It's a mournful happiness—you can tell the mood in the room drops—but there's still a kind of color to it.

CONTEXTUAL

JEFF
Was there anything that was unique to that church?

HANNAH
Well . . . prayer requests about people that belong to that church. Those are unique to each place.
(Pause. She's thinking.)
One lady standing near us kind of starting screaming, not because she was mad or crazy, but with passion for God. The choir director was really passionate too, moving around, and she had the biggest gestures I have ever seen. Even though she was middle-aged, it was almost like she was dancing when she was directing.

The choir had a special song to sing to visitors. They made us stand up, this island of high school kids in jeans in a sea of colorful outfits—lots of hats.

One thing I liked about that church is that even though they're bigger than our church, they took a couple of minutes during the greeting time instead of the fifteen seconds at our church. You could go around and meet new people and say hi to friends. At our church you only can shake hands with a couple of people near you, and then you're done.

COUNTER-CULTURAL

JEFF
Did anything happen that was sort of pushing back on the world, saying this worship is different than the culture around it?

HANNAH

One church in Omaha was mostly for homeless people. It was called something like The Empty Tomb. The majority of people there went downstairs after worship and got the free meal and the bag of groceries. I sat next to a guy who was starting a bilingual church in Texas. I don't remember what songs we sang.

CROSS-CULTURAL

HANNAH

It's cool hearing people's testimonies. Like when we went to the prison and heard those people's stories. A man in his 50s was in for dealing drugs; he said that this time had turned out to be different than the other times. And a woman, Kay, was in for second-degree manslaughter. She was happy the day we were there because she had a 24-hour release coming up—and she was going to go stay at her sister's. Everything she owned had to fit into this green tub. She put her sewing kit in her tub. It helped her with her depression. She kept saying, "It only takes one time." For something to change your life drastically.

JEFF

What else about your worship experiences has cut across cultures?

HANNAH

Well, they had a Spanish translator at the homeless church. She was a woman.

JEFF

Have the preachers at all the churches you've visited been men?

HANNAH

Yeah. The only woman speaking was the one who translated.

JEFF

I have a friend named Lin. She's on the worship leadership staff of a large church. She sometimes writes the words that the men say on the platform, but she's not permitted to stand on the platform and say the words herself. What do you think about that?

HANNAH

I don't know.

I think you will agree that there is no church where the tension is all resolved and everything is in balance. Perhaps it can be a bit of solace to acknowledge that we are called to work at a puzzle that is not actually fully solvable. As Thomas Long writes in *Testimony*:

> *Congregations are not just clubs or social cliques; they are to some degree microcosms of God's society, small mirrors of the diverse humanity whom God calls together. Even when congregations fight and split and get down to a handful of folks, "just like us," God has a way of sending a stranger, a visitor, and the diversity begins all over again.*

Struggles Over Pronouns

Christ for me, yes it's Christ for me,
He's my Savior, my Lord and king,
I'm so happy I shout and sing,
Christ for me, yes it's Christ for me,
Every day as I go my way it is Christ for me!
— A popular chorus
from the early twentieth century

It was Wednesday. Along with a divinity student named Amy, Karen and I were leading morning worship at the seminary. It was a very simple, very personal time.

Amy began by lighting a candle that rested on a small, round table along with a Bible, a crystal bowl of water, and a towel. She looked us in the eyes and said, "Love's never been like this. Love's never been so clear."

There were no musical instruments used that day. It was my job, from my place in the front row, to begin some songs. I chose songs that I hoped most of us could sing easily from memory. No song sheets, no power point, no hymn books, no instructions—I just started singing, and others joined. The congregation sang well. Some closed their eyes. Some raised their hands. Karen told me later that she saw many tears when she rose to present her meditation. She spoke from memory the following story:

On a sunny, windy spring morning, after I got my three kids off to their schools, I went for my morning walk around the golf course. I am finished with the rigors of my school schedule two weeks before my kids are, so that time is precious to me. It's just me, the wind, and my thoughts. It's good.

At the beginning of the path, I look carefully at the groomed gardens and flowerbeds to my right. The first yard has grapevines, apple trees, raspberries, vegetables, flowers. The man who lives there is a dentist in town. His wife works at the town library. They are the people I consult if I have questions about my own grapevine and raspberries. Their gardens inspire and motivate this farm girl, and I begin to think about my wildly unrealistic plans for my own yard this summer. The flowers on the balcony/porch of the second house make me smile. Colorful, careful, meticulous, reserved. I don't even aspire to such fastidiousness.

Right after the houses comes the swimming pool. I wonder if I should buy a family pass this year. I wonder if Daniel is old enough for me to send to the pool by himself this year. I wonder if Hannah and Daniel will do well in swimming lessons this year. I wonder if Hannah will speak up for herself this year and if Daniel will be able to listen carefully this year.

By the time I've walked the first mile, I'm out by the gravel road and I begin to let go of the daily concerns of my life. I have just lived through another Northwestern commencement. I say "lived through" because I wonder how many more I can go through without it being more than I can emotionally handle. All the goodbyes. My students become my kids. I try to love them fiercely. And they love me back. In four years they become my friends, and in fact, they are my only social life during the school year. But then comes the goodbye-ing. Each of them takes a piece of me with them. How many pieces can a heart break into?

I think about Kristin, who came to me a few weeks before school was out to say that she was pregnant and leaving school. Josh, who spent the year lying and manipulating himself out of responsibilities and will return next fall by the skin of his teeth. Leah, who is the embodiment of "outdoing one another in showing honor." Stacy, whose depression almost cost her her life. Lee, who got exactly the hotshot Santa Fe Opera internship he wanted. Jonathan, the ultra-efficient assistant, who drives himself and others crazy with his lists. Emily, who waited through weeks of tests in order to find out whether or not her mother had cancer. Pete, who is often the bright spot in my day because she always greets me with "Hi, beautiful!" Kristen and Nate, newlyweds dealing with Kristen's severe panic attacks with strong faith and fierce humor. Nick, who revealed his childhood sexual abuse in my speech class.

By now I'm walking across the entrance to the sub-division where the rich people are building their homes. My thoughts turn into prayers.

I pray that Daisy will finally see and own how truly gifted she is. I pray that Matt will allow himself some healthy anger. I pray that Nate will stop sabotaging his own work. I pray that Mary Beth's reason for transferring is not to run away.

I am stopped short by a sound I know well. Yes. A meadowlark. A song of my childhood. Meadowlarks are more scarce now where I grew up because much of the meadow has been planted as corn and soybeans. But for a split second I am back home.

I pray that Becky will know herself better. I pray that

Amanda's anger will be replaced with grace.

I am at the clubhouse now. Not being, nor having any desire to be, a golfer, I very briefly wonder exactly what goes on in a clubhouse. The wind seems especially fierce. I meet an older gentleman who has just entered the trail. He is walking his bicycle and as we meet, he shakes his head and says, "I'm alright going with the wind, but I'm not worth a hoot against it." I smile and nod and say, "Yes. I know what you mean."

I think about Ryan, to whom I had to apologize before he graduated so that I wouldn't forever be embarrassed when I thought of him or saw him. Dan, whose mother died just as school began last fall. Brian, who crucified me in my student course evaluations. Sara, who has huge dreams. How do I help her find the strength of her inner voice? Tonya, who is forever doubting her call to her art. How do I tell her to stop listening to her parents and her church and listen instead to the voice of the Spirit in her life? How will I like it when a college professor tells my kid that same thing?

I round the corner and am suddenly on the edge of a grove of trees. There is absolutely no sound but the wind in the trees. For a few precious seconds, there are no houses within my range of vision. No people. No roads. It is, again, a feeling of my childhood. A feeling of belonging. A feeling of being able to escape to a place where no one will intrude on my thoughts or my time. And I suddenly break down weeping. And the intensity of the emotion surprises me. I had not realized how lonely I was. How utterly spent.

Lord, are you sure this is where you want me? I never imagined this is where I'd end up. Couldn't I do something else? Something less, well, less emotionally draining? Something that includes time for my garden. Space

for my birds. Listening to wind. Maybe even a ham-
mock? This is hard. Awfully hard. I finish the three miles,
and I turn onto the street toward home. The old man's
words ring in my ears: "I'm alright going with the wind,
but I'm not worth a hoot against it."

I know, Lord, I know. My call is crystal clear. I know
that.

The wind picks up again, and I feel it, strong and sure,
against my back.

You can imagine why this meditation on calling would be
meaningful to students buried under the busyness of seminary.
Karen ended the time of worship urging us to take with us
words from the book that we love:

I press on to take hold of that for which
Christ Jesus took hold of me.

(Philippians 3:12b)

After chapel, there was evidence, in the tears and the words
of gratitude, that chapel had been a meaningful time for many
of the worshipers present.

Fifteen minutes later, we were sitting having coffee and one
of the seminary's retired professors came over to our table. He
said he would like to share some criticism. He reminded us that
the seminary's international students could not participate unless we provided lyrics for the songs. He then said, "Many of the
professors were also not singing because those songs are not a
part of our tradition."

We thanked him for his feedback, but I continued to wonder throughout that day about his comment that many of the
professors were not singing. I could tell by the sound in the

room that most people there were singing. Were they all students? And what of the last words he had said, "... those songs are not a part of our tradition"? Surely this man of God was not complaining about learning new songs. Was there a deeper concern?

Two days later, this same retired professor came back into our life. Tim had invited him to give a guest lecture on John Calvin in the worship class that Karen, Tim, and I were team teaching. Late in the lecture, our guest said, "One of the reasons that Calvin wanted to sing only Psalms was to avoid the 'Jesus and me' theology that is present in so many of our songs today. Now, I'm all for new songs, and I know that faith must, in part, be personal. I enjoyed singing 'Christ for me!' when I was a boy. But I've had to give that up, because Christ is not just for me."

I thought back to the chapel that we had led two days earlier. Sure enough, there it was. The first person pronoun was all over the place. "My Jesus, my Savior ... ," "Purify my heart ... ," "Jesus loves me. ... ."

A light bulb went on. Perhaps what the retired professor had meant by "not part of our tradition" was more specifically a difference in pronoun preference. I grew up in the "Jesus and me" tradition. I sang "Christ for me" as a child. Like the retired professor, I do not sing that song anymore (its musical style feels outdated now), but I still sing, "... that saved a wretch like me."

Two more days went by, and it was Sunday. Our family visited a new church. Surprise. The retired professor met us in the narthex. We had stumbled into his worship home.

Sure enough, the first hymn was filled with third person pronouns. No "I" or "me" anywhere. We sang:

We strain to glimpse your mercy seat
And find you kneeling at our feet.

I stood in worship that Sunday asking myself what was wrong with me. Why was my heart strangely chilled? Would I rather have sung:

I strain to glimpse your mercy seat
And find you kneeling at my feet.

Am I opposed to songs using third person pronouns? No, I told myself, that is not it. I readily sing:

You are the One that we praise
You are One we adore
You give the healing and grace our
Hearts always hunger for,
Oh our hearts always hunger for.

I guess I am not certain what was wrong with me that Sunday morning. Perhaps it was the imagery of the kneeling, servant Christ. I wondered why such a solitary image was used alongside a group pronoun. But who am I to criticize Brian Wren, the world-renowned writer of those lyrics? Indeed, that is not my intent here. I am simply telling you that on that Sunday morning I found myself wondering if Wren's tradition or values urged him to lean toward the third person pronoun. Sure enough, I discovered a *Christian Century* interview from May of 2000 in which Wren observes:

Many people hunger for some sense of personal contact with the divine, a contact that involves the heart as well as the head. That is entirely valid, although it's unwise to be too confident that what you feel is the divine. But the negative side to this search is that it can become a pre-occupation with "my own journey, my own feelings," as if they were unique and quite separate from everybody else's.... A lot of Christian worship is too inward-turned, too nostalgic or escapist. That inwardness can mean that we focus only on ourselves....

Ah ha. It was not really the song that I was having trouble with. What was wrong with me was that I was having the same trouble as the retired seminary professor. I was sensing two traditions colliding.

You have probably recognized this tension over little words in your own worship experience. It is likely that you worship in a tradition that tends toward "I" or tends toward "we." The two traditions are in agreement that God is to be the primary focus of our worship, but we accomplish this goal by different uses of personal pronouns. Church historian Lester Ruth is hinting at the two traditions in the following passage from his essay "A Rose By Any Other Name":

> *One could also look at how the congregation explains the meaning of baptism and the Lord's Supper. Are these events about each individual's personal experience of a gracious God who has given us life abundant, or are they signs by which, to use the language of the newest United Methodist baptismal service, we are "incorporated into God's mighty acts of salvation."*

My mother's experience of the Lord's Supper is firmly within Professor Ruth's first description of an "individual personal experience." I seldom come to communion without glancing down the pew, wherever I am, and seeing my mother in tears. It happened every week the golden plate was passed during my formative years. Why was my mother crying? She would say she was having a divine encounter. As John Witvliet writes in *Worship Seeking Understanding*:

> . . . *worshipers in nearly every Christian tradition experience some of what happens in worship as divine encounter. Differences in Christian worship arise not so much whether or not God is understood to be present, but rather in what sense.*

For people in my mother's tradition, there is a "Yes, me, too, count me in" quality to corporate worship. Such worship is often accompanied by great emotion, and it is personal. That is the tradition in which I came to faith and became a worshiper. But now I have wandered in and among several other traditions. What can be done to bring these disparate traditions together? I have found much to celebrate in every corner of the kingdom of Christ. But what pronouns shall be used? Must we use only one or the other? How can one say the Lord's Prayer without "we"? How can one speak or sing a testimony without "I"? Must there be continuing accusations of inadequate theology and continuing separate worshiping communities over these little words?

One thing I find especially hopeful about the Reformed tradition is that it affirms continuing reformation by the Spirit of God. May God continue to reform us, you and me.

"Thank You" Is a Beautiful Story

One sixth century monk, Dorotheus of Gaza, describes detach-
ment as "being free from [wanting] certain things to happen,"
and remaining so trusting of God that "what is happening will
be the thing you want and you will be at peace with all"
— Kathleen Norris
Amazing Grace

While on sabbatical, Karen and I moved with our kids into the Chicago neighborhood known as Logan Square. We lived at the corner of Fullerton and Kimball. When we first moved there, I threw my satchel over my shoulder and went prowling the neighborhood for coffee shops. I had an agenda. I was looking for a place to write. My first stop was Johnny's Grill. It is a busy place with cheap food, but you do not want to linger there. The sign above the grill says, "You'll have it my way. This isn't Burger King." Eat and get out. My next stop was a place to linger, recently named "Best Breakfast in Chicago." But the prices were for tourists, not for writers. And the wait staff was too good—they actually waited on you. Writers prefer more inattention than attention. That place was not to be my morning home. McDonalds was up Milwaukee, but they want you gone in thirty minutes or less, and the second cup of coffee is not free. I kept looking.

It took me about a week to find "Click on Café." It was five blocks straight west of us on Fullerton. The owners had spent the past winter transforming an old beer garden. Now they had a breakfast and lunch café with a bright, clean look. It was an oasis on the border between old Chicago and Mexico. Cuban sandwiches were their lunch specialty, but they also served great breakfasts, freshly cooked by the man who had handcrafted all the woodwork in the place. The owner had quit his job as a graphic artist so that he and his wife could join together in this new venture of coffee shop, computer café. I had found my writing home. I learned their names, and they learned mine. I learned the names of their children, and they learned mine. I guessed that they were Christians, and sure enough, we spotted them at one of the churches we visited. We had become members of the same neighborhood.

It was a new business, and I was one of the few regular customers. They took good care of me. They let me sit quietly all morning with my laptop. They let me plug my laptop in when the battery ran out. They missed me when I was not there, and they shook my hand when I returned.

One Sunday I brought my family to the café after church. Some of us ordered lunch, and some of us ordered late breakfast. As I paid, the owner said, "How were the omelets?" Remembering the proverb, "The wounds of a friend are better than the kisses of an enemy," I said, "My wife asked that you leave out the peppers and onions. You also left out the tomatoes."

"I'm sorry," said the owner. "I won't charge you for that one."

"No, no, no!" I exclaimed, "You charge me. Charge me extra! You do a lot for me—you let me sit in here whole mornings. I just thought you would want to know the truth."

The next morning, the owner saw me coming up the street

and had my coffee at my table as I was entering the door. He said, "I'm sorry about yesterday. Olga doesn't know English and sometimes she gets things wrong. It was four times this past week. We're going to hire a new girl from church, one who knows Spanish and English." He went off to get my breakfast, and I sat there wondering if I had cost Olga her job. I had simply answered a question about an omelet. I had not accused Olga. I was trying to say thank you. Just then, Olga arrived for work. I said, "*Hola.*" That is one of the few Spanish words I know. She went back to take off her coat. The owner returned with my food. I said to him, "You know it wasn't Olga who took our order yesterday. It was the young man who speaks English. He didn't mean to make a mistake. He's just learning. I've made lots of mistakes in my life. I just thought you would want to know the truth."

"He's a good boy," said the owner, "He's my son's friend."

I went back to my laptop and my breakfast. Olga came out with a broom. The owner said, "Olga." She turned. He held out a full coffee cup to her. She smiled with surprise. She walked over and took the cup in both of her hands. She said, "*Gracias.*"

It was a beautiful moment.

Every Lord's Day brings with it missed attempts and false starts. Sometimes this might cause us to overlook what is right there in front of us—the simple beauty of people giving gifts and saying thank you.

Not Every Story Is Happy

Worship is, as I have said, a key element in the church's "language school" for life. The point is not to go through life speaking in a "stained glass voice." The point is to let the language of worship shape our witness outside of the sanctuary.

— Thomas Long
Testimony

Are worship leaders language teachers?

A worship project called "Vertical Habits" started at River Community Church in Edmonton, Alberta. Then in early fall of 2005, the Calvin Institute of Christian Worship took the project a step further by inviting a number of churches and writers from throughout North America to apply this concept within their worship communities. That fall our church joined the project.

The premise here is that worship is vertical—it is between us and God. And worship is a habit—a discipline—something we do whether we feel like it or not. Worship is, thus, a vertical habit.

Vertical? It is true that God is not only above us, but beside us, within us and supporting us. But we can readily agree that a common biblical image for relating with God is to look up.

I lift up my eyes to you,
  To you whose throne is in heaven.
                    (Psalm 123:1)

And when Jesus was baptized, he went up immediately
from the water, and behold, the heavens were opened
and he saw the Spirit of God descending like a dove, and
alighting on him . . .
                    (Matthew 3:16, RSV)

Since, then, you have been raised with Christ, set your
hearts on things above, where Christ is seated at the right
hand of God.
                    (Colossians 3:1)

After this I looked, and there before me was a door stand-
ing open in heaven. And the voice I had first heard speak-
ing to me like a trumpet said, "Come up here . . ."
                    (Revelation 4:1)

The word vertical is a reminder that worship is about an encounter with God.

Habit? What sort of habit? As I mentioned earlier, worship is one of the spiritual disciplines, but the Vertical Habits
project intends to focus on a specific type of discipline: communication. We communicate with God in worship. We approach God to say a variety of things. These communication
patterns are basic to relationships, like:

"I love you."
"I'm wrong and I'm sorry."
"Thank you."
"I need help."

"My heart is breaking."
"I'll do whatever you ask."
"You're wonderful!"

The Bible teaches us that God wants to receive these messages from us. Each one of the above is a common theme in the Bible's prayer book, the Psalms. Each one of the above habits should be part of a balanced worship life. If worship is truly God's language school, then we are learning this balanced Godward communication during corporate worship, and what we learn in corporate worship, we carry into our private worship. And vice versa.

One of the core values of the Vertical Habits project was to restore breadth to our worship communication. At my home church, our assessment was that our church was fairly good at saying to God, "Thank you," and "I'll do whatever you ask." These are easy for us because we are polite in our town. We say please and thank you. And we are helpers. We are like the Iowans in *The Music Man*:

> *We'll give you our shirt and a back to go with it.*

But ours is an "emotions-close-to-the-chest" culture; we are not as good at saying, "I'm wrong and I'm sorry," or "My heart is breaking," or even "You're wonderful!" In other words, true confession, passionate lament, and giddy celebration are not common experiences in this Dutch-heritage town.

Okay, now we had identified a more difficult problem than we thought. It was not only a problem of worship being out of balance, but it was a problem of our very culture being out of balance. We did not know where the problem started, but we knew that if we were going to have a breadth of communication with God, we needed to practice a breadth of communication with one another. It needed to cut both ways.

What could we do? We decided to tell stories.

We created a collection of stories (one or two stories for every single day of the seven weeks) that reflected the seven "vertical habits" that we had selected (adoration, confession, thanksgiving, supplication, lament, submission and celebration). Here is how we did it. I asked a group of about thirty writers in our congregation to get together on a Saturday morning and write personal stories. These stories must be, I told them, experiences from their own lives. I fed them mid-morning snacks and lunch. I gave them topics from the habits list, but as in the earlier chapter called "Story Pictures in Worship" I asked them not to mention God unless it was crucial to telling their story. I did not want a batch of mini-sermons. I wanted stories about a certain type of communication. I was hoping to remind us all that even in this quiet little town, we had a variety of things to say to each other. Once we could embrace that simple truth, I hoped we could acknowledge with the biblical writers that we also had a variety of things to say to God, even if we had not been saying them in public worship for a long, long time.

The writing team came up with such a variety of stories. They were as mundane and beautiful as the stories you will find in your own congregation. I assigned to each of the seven weeks one habit, and I assigned each day of the week at least one story. I put a Psalm on Sunday. The Psalms corresponded with a sermon series reminding us why we were focusing on these habits of communication with God. The stories reminded us that this sort of talk needs to be practiced with one another as well as with God. I asked the congregation to try not to read ahead—to read only the pages for each day. Some confessed that they cheated. We called the booklet *In the Habit of Faith*. Its goal was to change our culture and our worship. Would you like to see what I mean? Here you go.

"I love you." (adoration)

February 13, post-season tournament trail
Game one
Second quarter
I think it's doable
We have a half-time lead
Three minutes to go
I gently quiet the premature celebration by one of our players
Honor the opponent
Nervous energy anticipates the sure outcome
The pleasure of winning
Dreaming of the road to the state tournament

February 14, Valentine's Day
Floral and candy deliveries arrive at many office cubicles
A phone call arrives at mine
There was an accident
"It doesn't look good," the voice says
I had heard these words once before
Grandpa died then
Dad died today
The anguish of loss
Five hours on the road home

February 15, go through the motions
Buy a dark suit
Unfamiliar food in my familiar house
Funeral home and the visitation
"My sympathies to you"

"I'm so sorry"
"If there's anything we can do"
Thank you . . . thank you . . . thank you
They win two games in my absence
On the road back to life, work and games

February 19, back in the gym
Prepare for regional finals
I say a few words
They don't know how to respond
But they listen more intently than they have all season
One player finds me later
"I love you, coach," she says inside our hug
We win the game
They cut down the net and we take a team photo
The week comes flooding back
From funeral to hype so soon
I distance myself
Back to my seat on the front row of bleachers
"Here, coach, we want you to have the game ball
We'll all sign it in practice tomorrow"
Still on the road

> *Shirley Folkerts, 44, teacher and former six-girl*
> *defensive basketball coach at Pella Christian High School*
> *Reflecting back upon February of 1990*

"I'm wrong and I'm sorry." (confession)

I have a long history of being jarred awake by the tele-
phone. In my experience, people who call before 8 a.m.
seldom do so with good news. When I was in college, it
was my aunt calling to say my mother had had a heart

attack. When I was a young English professor, it was my entire composition class calling to ask, "Why aren't you here giving us the final exam??"

This morning it was Pastor Ron. "Michael," he boomed in his pedal-bass voice, "are you on your way to church?" Opening my eyes, I saw the clock read 7:59. Why would I be on my way to church at this—and then it hit me, like a blow to the body. The elements. This was my Sunday to set up for communion.

"I'm on my way, Ron," I lied, ripping off the covers and stumbling toward the closet. My mind was already thumbing through the refrigerator for something resembling grape juice. Not only had I forgotten to set up communion, you see, I had forgotten to purchase the juice and order the bread. And in our small Iowa town the grocery store does not open on Sunday. No grape juice, I confirmed, as my body caught up with my mind in the kitchen. Concentrate—the freezer! Pink lemonade, orange juice . . . "This is my Raspberry-Banana-Peach juice, shed for you . . . ??" I pictured the pink liquid in the tray of tiny cups.

What about the bread, the host, the symbol of Christ's sacrifice? In the cupboards—wheat thins, graham crackers, Ritz Bits. On the counter—half a loaf of Wonder Bread. Will it be enough for 75 people?

Ten minutes later, I burst through the church doors with my Wonder Bread and Juicy Juice. Linens, trays, cups, platters, chalice—and the service starts in ten minutes! The communion cups seem impossibly small to my shaking hands. I have managed to fill about a dozen when I hear for the second time, "Michael." It is Pastor Ron, and I hear the smile in his voice before I see it on his face. His deep voice is calm. "Michael, it's time for church. We'll have communion next week. No big deal."

"OK," I answer, lying still. No big deal?? Failing in my duties as an elder, depriving a congregation of the Eucharist, interfering with the sacrament of Holy Communion!

With my mind full of the groceries of worship, I am not prepared to attend worship. I cannot face the people I have let down. Grabbing my coat from the kitchen counter, I slip back out the door into the stinging winter air.

January in northwest Iowa is lifeless and bleak. Fields which held rows of corn and soybeans now lie stubbly and bare. Through the fields stretch endless gravel roads, arrow-straight but for the curvature of the earth.

I drive fast, away from, not towards. Each minute puts another mile between me and my failure. Each mile makes the faces of the congregation a little smaller.

After thirty miles I begin to smile. My life is back there in that place with those people. My family is sitting on the third pew on the left, wondering where I am. Where I am is traveling in the wrong direction on the road to forgiveness.

Calmer now, I slow the car for a U-turn on the icy road. My mind is already with my family in the warm sanctuary. As I turn, my car slides off the road and into the icy ditch. "Of course," I say to the wheel, "running away is easy, going home is hard."

Cat litter. "Cat litter," I can hear my wife saying. "Always keep a bag of cat litter in your trunk for emergencies. Sprinkle it onto the ice for better traction." Popping the trunk, I confirm my suspicion. There is no cat litter in my car. More than that, I have forgotten my gloves. I can picture them lying on the counter beside the communion chalice.

My fingers are numb when I finally succeed in digging

the front wheels of my car. I speed back along the desolate road with the heater blasting, my fingers jammed into the vents.

The service has ended, but Pastor Ron is still there. "Michael," I hear for the third time today, "we missed you in church this morning."

"I know," I say. "I'm sorry."

"It's all right," he answers. "Welcome back."

Michael Kensak, 34, professor, choir director
a worshiper with cat litter in his trunk

"Thank you." (thanksgiving)

Feeling rested for the first time in weeks, I made my way along the Iowa highways back to school after a much needed midterm break. It was good to see my family again. I did have a twinge of guilt for not coming home at all that semester even though I only lived a few hours away. But, "I was a senior," I told myself, "I've got to become more independent." My thoughts quickly went back to myself as I looked ahead to the rest of the semester, knowing that the hardest part was still in front of me.

A few days later I received a phone call. I stood outside in the brisk evening air so that the cell phone could get reception. My sister, a freshman at the same college, stood with me. She is an emotional person and tends to worry by nature so she was already worked up when our mom called and said she needed to talk to us both. I remember hearing the words my mother spoke and feeling as if I were in a movie or in some dream that I would abruptly awake from. "When your dad was in surgery they found cancer," she said. "They have removed as much as they could, but they couldn't get it all."

I had never experienced such total and utter heartache. We went down to my room, and I held my sister as she wept. It wasn't until she finally left that I released my own agony in a stream of tears.

In this utter state of helplessness, I was blown away by the love of others. That night my roommate stayed up till the late hours of the morning with me, just praying next to me. My girlfriend held me and expressed, without words that she was there for me. People began writing emails, letters and postcards to let me know that they were concerned and praying for my dad and my family. People went out of their way to make sure I was okay. While I didn't find much relief in their words, I found peace in their presence. Letters came from Georgia, Wisconsin, and even Texas—all places that I had lived years ago. Several members of our church sent gas cards so I could drive home, and one lady sent me a roll of quarters so that I could do laundry.

That Thanksgiving was very different. As our family gathered around the table and thanked God for his many blessings, I felt overwhelmed. I felt that if I had spent that whole day just thanking God, at the end of the day I wouldn't have spoken of my gratitude. My dad ate the little bit of turkey that he could, and then fell asleep in his armchair watching football. I never thought that I would be so happy to hear him snore.

Andy Keller, 22, college student
My dad, a pastor, is currently battling his cancer,
and even though his hair is falling out from the chemo,
he has still been preaching on Sundays.

"I need help." (supplication)

Frances slowly lowered herself to the floor; a dish pan and cloth close by her side. At ninety years old this was no easy task, but she longed to be of service to the young mother who had recently moved with her husband and newborn daughter from Arlington, Virginia to Omaha, Nebraska—1,300 miles from parents in Pennsylvania. The young mother was me, and I felt both grateful and chagrined watching her. "I should be the one scrubbing the floor," I thought, but she insisted.

As a first time mom reeling in the haze of sleeplessness, cleaning my apartment was the last thing on a long list of thing to do. Not that it wasn't on my mind, ever nagging, but rarely getting done. It seemed more important, however, to figure out how to get a shower from time to time. Simple tasks like going to the store or doing laundry in the communal laundry room overwhelmed me as I tried to do them with a baby in tow. Since we had only one car, the baby and I spent lots of time together in the car driving my husband back and forth to work, a twenty minute drive one way. When I had a quiet moment, cleaning was the last thing I wanted to do. I was lonely; I wanted to connect with people.

Frances was lonely, too. Our friendship began with a wave. Actually, it was my visiting aunt who waved, but that didn't seem to matter to Frances who was grateful for the simple gesture. A few days after the wave, I crossed the lawn that separated our apartments to introduce myself to the slight woman with stooped shoulders whom I watched daily as she swept her patio and watered her beautiful flowers. I introduced myself and told her how much I enjoyed looking across at her colorful patio. She introduced herself and asked how the baby was doing, a sign that she watched me just as I had been watching her.

I learned much of Frances' life story in that brief encounter. She was a widow of about 15 years. Her husband died after they had been married 63 years. She thanked me for waving to her a few days prior. I told her that was my aunt. She said that in the six months she had lived in her apartment, no one had greeted her. The only interactions she had were with family members who would come to check on her. She wanted a friend. She wanted to be a friend. As we parted she said, "You come again and bring that baby." It was almost a command.

I did go back and I did bring the baby. She fed me warm buttered toast and a cup of chocolate while she held the baby who fell asleep in her arms. I enjoyed the break and our conversation. Often she would call me up and command me to come over or announce that she was coming over. That was her way. She showed her love with food and by entertaining the baby. Again and again she fed me and, later, the baby—pudding, cookies, soup, enchiladas, fruit. She wanted to do more. One day she told me that she was going to come over to help me clean.

What was I to do? How could I accept the help of this dear woman? I knew she wasn't insulting me by offering to help. Part of me was glad for the offer but another part of me resisted. Maybe I could have her dust or perhaps hold the baby while I cleaned. She had other ideas. She was going to clean my kitchen and my bathrooms and to her that meant getting down on her hands and knees to scrub the floor. I let her. Because we were friends.

Samantha Winn, 35, wife and homemaker
mother of three children

"My heart is breaking." (lament)

The time had come in the worship service for the Children's Sermon.

As the preacher, I didn't look forward to this. It's a tough assignment. Not many preachers, including me, know really how to talk to kids. It's not easy. I was always glad when it was finished. I think the kids were also.

As I invited the kids to come to the front of the church today, some came running, others were pulled along by an older brother or sister or parent. Their enthusiasm brought joy to my heart. I prayed silently, "Lord, I don't know how to talk to these kids, but please don't let me destroy their enthusiasm." Then I noticed something. Jacob was very quiet. He was always so bubbly. Today he looked sad.

I was about to begin my little talk when Jacob said, "Mister, do you believe in doggie heaven?" I was silent. That's not my nature. I am usually very quick to answer any question without thinking. This time I waited. With tears rolling down his cheeks he softly said, "My dog died this week, he was hit by a car." I choked up. Now what do I say? I don't know how, but I know God told me, "Don't say anything stupid." Then two words came to me. I know they came from God. I put my arm around Jacob and whispered, "I'm sorry."

*Rev. Don Den Hartog, 72, retired pastor
remembering a day at his last pastorate*

"I'll do whatever you ask." (submission)

When I was first married, my husband and I moved to Santa Barbara, California. It was the first of many adventures we would take together. I got a job right away in an entry level position at a life insurance office. It was my first real, full time job, and while I didn't hate it, it wasn't my favorite place to be.

After about two years I went to work feeling excited for the first time in a long while. Today my boss was going to announce the new manager of the underwriting staff department and the job had my name written all over it. I'd been in the department for two years. I was pleasant. I worked over time. I picked up slack. I was ready!

My excitement was replaced with a rock in my stomach as I saw someone else sitting in what I had started to consider "my" chair and "my" desk. I was filled with indignation as my boss casually announced the new manager (who wasn't me) and went quietly back into her office and shut the door.

Shaking, I went to my own desk and pretended to take a phone call to avoid eye contact with the people I'd already told about my supposed promotion. In my head I was shouting, "She's been here six months! She takes long lunches! She was sloppy drunk at the company party! Not fair, not fair, not fair!"

It didn't take me long to change from hard working and cheerful to resentful and moody. If I had a task I didn't like, everyone knew it. If my new manager gave me an assignment, I was ready with a chilly response and a determination to pawn the job onto someone else. Gone was the gal everyone could depend on to get the job done. I went to work to collect the pay check and nothing else.

After three months of this, I was called into the boss's

office. (Actually, I was surprised I hadn't been called in sooner.) I was told to shape up or find a new place of employment. I was told the raise that I expected would not come, and I was being placed on probation. I was humiliated.

I left early that day and had the weekend to adjust my attitude. I decided to go to work on Monday more like my old self. It was not an easy day.

I went to my manager first thing that morning and explained myself. I told her I was sorry about my resentment and that I would make an effort to do better.

She promptly thanked me and handed me a stack of files that would keep me too busy to pout. Her eyes glittered with the unspoken words, "Prove it."

The decision to give up my pride made my life easier. Once my mind was made up, my heart easily followed. I found myself breathing a little better, and my co-workers started inviting me to lunch again.

I never did get a promotion, but I did make a friend of the manager. I find that when I look back at that time I understand why I wasn't chosen for the job. It doesn't sting like it did. My experience makes a difference in how I respond to disappointment now.

Amy Anderson, 37, wife and mom
still learning about submission

"You're wonderful!" (celebration)

Mom nearly had a heart attack last week—they called it a pending heart attack. Dad took her to the hospital where the doctor looked at the first ECG and said to my mom, "Dr. Rukhsana, you're being paranoid. You're fine, go home." But mom refused, she knew. They did the test again. The doctor, looking at the latest results, turned gray at the thought of what he had nearly done. . . .

Now here we were—five days since mom had insisted on staying at the hospital. We don't really know what's going on. Dad came by to make sure we were okay, "Millie, Nicky, take care of the younger ones...." There had been a steady stream of aunties from church who had looked in on us; the kitchen counters were piled high with dinners—rice, curry, lots of good things. One aunty had come and done the laundry. It is quiet now; the four of us sit in the living room. Dad had called, the operation was done, "Eat dinner, feed Abhi and Esther, I'll be home soon. No, don't worry about mummy."

Mummy was so young, she couldn't have heart problems. Everything had happened so fast and seemed unreal. What would life be like after this? Would Millie and I have to take care of all the things mom...how would we? I think about the food in the kitchen and wonder, how many days it would be before Millie and I would have to start cooking.

Finally Millie picks up a video mummy had brought home from the library—six days ago. She reads the cover, "'A Room with a View' based on the novel by E. M. Forster." It sounds terribly boring but we just sit there in the darkening living room and watch the movie, lethargically and unemotionally.

Suddenly the four of us gasp—one of the characters in the movie has just begun running around naked! Here comes another one, and another. "It's the preacher, Nicky!" We start screaming. Esther and Abhi jump up and down as I try to grab their heads and make them close their eyes, Millie grabs the remote control to press "stop" but instead, presses "slow." We watch for a moment *in horrified silence as three men run, in slow motion, around a pool, very naked; and then we start shrieking louder. Millie, her fingers shaking from laughing, can't press the right button so she drops the remote control and joins me; we try to clasp our hands over our siblings' eyes. They defiantly evade our clutches and we chase them around the living room, we're all jumping and shrieking and laughing because . . . that's all we can do. We laugh and scream and laugh . . . and then there's a knock at the door.*

We fall silent and look at each other. We're terrible children. Our mother is in the hospital and could be dying and here we're laughing! What would the person at the door think? We all go to the door, quietly, and I open it. Standing outside is Malliga, aunty from church, she's wearing a lavender cotton sari and holding a big dish of chicken curry in her hands. Her eyes are curious but she's smiling, "What's happening here?"

I'm the only one who can speak, "Aunty, we were just . . . laughing," I explain weakly. Her smile gets bigger, "And so you should children, you should laugh."

We dissolve into each other—giggling, exhausted and relieved and tell the aunty what happened. After she leaves, Abhi, Esther, and I tease Millie, "You pressed 'slow motion' on purpose."

Hephzibah "Nicky" Dutt, 22, college student
My mom is home in Oman, and she's doing fine.

The seven weeks' worth of stories in the booklet *In the Habit of Faith* ended with these words:

Our seven weeks are already gone. I don't know about you, but I want the stories to continue. I hope we'll find ways to encourage the sharing of stories in our worship services, along with the remembering of the Psalms. And also along with the practicing of the sort of things that we've been saying here. One last story might serve to encourage us all as to the importance of living lives of adoration, confession, thanksgiving, supplication, lament, submission and celebration.

The diagnosis was a death sentence—lung cancer. It was June when we found out. By Thanksgiving, my father would be gone. But we didn't know that yet, and on this July day we went to the farm—my siblings and our spouses and our children—so that we could cry together and pray together and plan together and hope together. So that we could love our parents well. The phone rang and I answered it. The voice on the other end belonged to my parents' pastor. He asked for my mom, and then said, "Karen, wait. Since I've got you on the phone, tell me how your parents are really doing." I paused, hoping I could find words that would match what I observed in them. "You know, pastor, they're fine. I mean, they're hurting, of course. But they've spent their whole lives preparing for this. So, they're fine."

When I was a little girl, I remember telling my mother that I was afraid to die. She told me not to worry about it; that God gives you the grace to die when the time comes, not before. But what I learned that summer and fall was that the grace to die comes because of a life lived in the habit of faith.

Karen Bohm Barker, 53, college professor
grateful daughter

Stories Have Soundtracks

Praise him with the sound of the trumpet:
praise him with the psaltery and harp.
Praise him with the timbrel and dance:
praise him with stringed instruments and organs.
Praise him upon the loud cymbals:
praise him upon the high sounding cymbals.
— Psalm 150:3–5, KJV

When I was in high school, it seemed as if everyone played the guitar. Except me. I was in plays, in the high school choir, and on the tennis team. I did not have time for a garage band. In fact, I heard sermons against rock and roll. Syncopated rhythms, they told us, would lead to "unwanted pregnancy." Our little church would not have dreamed of allowing a guitar on the platform. One boy in our youth group played guitar in a band. His fatal error was to go public. His band cut a single which had an original ballad on one side and a cover of "Roll Over Beethoven" on the flip side. Once I was delivering newspapers near his house, and I saw the pastor going in. I heard later that the pastor told the son he could no longer be a member of the church if he continued to play in the band. After that, the whole family quit coming to church. Some people said, "See what rock and roll causes."

I was too young and too confused to mount a response. I was busy trying to decide if dancing and going to movies were really as evil as everyone at my church said. My world was pre-cyberspace small. I had not yet heard of Larry Norman and "Why Does the Devil Get All the Good Music?" I had not read C. S. Lewis or seen a picture of him sitting in a pub with a pint.

Our church had an electric organ always played by Florence Bentley and a piano always played by Mary Alice Cross. Those two instruments were used pretty much every Sunday morning. Sometimes Mr. Erickson would bring his trombone and play along with the singing, doing an occasional, showy, full-octave slide and that, for me, was a pretty exciting Sunday.

Then I went away to college and my world exploded. I learned that Christ's church had existed before 1961 when the group that founded our church began holding prayer meetings in the old auto body shop. I learned that the King James was neither the first nor the last Bible translation. I heard speaking in tongues for the first time. I read *Mere Christianity*.

And I bought a guitar.

Within three years, I would pay my final visit to my home church. My parents moved to California, so I had no reason to return. We had all moved away physically, but I also just moved away, attempting to learn respect for the wide world of worshipers. I now know that this journey will never be complete, and I also have come to realize that this journey strangely still includes that little group of believers that nurtured my childhood faith and also my narrow-mindedness.

Thirty years have gone by since I bought my first guitar. I am worship coordinator at a church that has guitar stands scattered on the platform—spaces for acoustic, electric and bass. There is a drum set and a double-rack synthesizer. There is a sixteen-year-old sax player at our church whose riffs would leave Mr. Erickson slack-jawed. There is cello and violin. There is a piano. There is a choir. There are singers galore.

There is a pipe organ.

For thousands of Sundays, the pipe organ in this Iowa church was the only instrument you would have heard. The organist was essentially the song leader. Not now. Not anymore. This change is to be expected, since the local climate has changed. There is more diversity in our town than there has been since it was founded by Dutch immigrants in the 1870s. This diversity is reflected in the instruments we play and the songs we sing. Unless theologically prohibited (as my home church thought about guitars), worship leaders work with the instruments that the worshipers play. And they sing songs in a style appropriate to the people in the pew—you do not typically hear sitars in Iowa worship services, but someday soon you may be hearing more Spanish guitars in my church. The culture is changing in many ways, and these changes have impacted the use of the organ. Our church and many similar churches across the land are asking, "What is the role of the organ in worship?" The very fact that this question is being asked suggests change is in the wind. Change always means that something will be lost as something else is gained. And loss is always accompanied by grief.

One recent Sunday morning, I was the worship coordinator. Someone else was leading, but I was there in a supportive role. I arose at my usual predawn time and walked the worship space double-checking its readiness for the sacred activity of the day. Eventually, the team gathered and checked mics and stands and instruments and sheet music and cues.

The organist was sitting quietly, waiting. She is a woman who has served worship by pressing those foot pedals for many decades of her life. She once told me that when she started attending this church, she was not allowed to play because the organist slots were all taken. It took her a long time to earn a place on the bench. But she is still the church's youngest organist today, and she is in her late sixties.

She seemed especially still this morning, so I slid down the pew and broached the subject of her mood, "Good morning. How are you doing?" She and I have learned to trust each other, so she gave me a straight up response. She said, "This is my last Sunday playing the organ." What? Did I hear correctly? I said, "What do you mean?" She told me that she had not told anyone yet, but, she said, "I've had one too many rehearsals in which the role of the organ was unclear."

I was having flashbacks to the tensions over music in my childhood church, only now we were playing the flip side. I also flashed back to a sermon tape I had heard in which a mega-church pastor asked, "How many seekers listen to organ music in their cars?"

But this was no time for glibness. I was sitting next to a woman who represented a lifetime of service to the worshiping community and she had just said to me, "This is my last Sunday playing the organ." It was a moment for listening.

I could see that the rehearsal run-through of the service was about to begin. "Will you meet me back on this pew immediately after church?" I whispered. She looked at me with tears in her eyes and said, "Yes."

After church we sat there together. I listened to her grieving heart. As she spoke, a middle-aged woman gently stepped up to the organ. "Excuse me," she said. "I don't mean to interrupt. But would you mind if I played the organ? I used to live here, and this is the organ I learned on. I'd love to play it again." We nodded our heads, and she slid onto the bench. We sat silently and listened. She played beautifully. When she finished, I said, "Do you come back often?" She shook her head. "No, not anymore." She slipped quickly away, wanting to catch up to those waiting for her. I did not even get her name.

I asked our organist not to quit while her emotions were running high, and she agreed that she would not. Two months later she tendered her resignation.

I once asked a friend who is a concert organist, "If you were looking for a new church, would you look for one with an organ?" She shocked me by saying no. She explained, "It's a special congregation that can afford an organ and can support its use."

The church is not about carpet or pews or pianos or organs or drums or guitars. These are all instruments for glorifying God. The church building itself is only a tool. One day, the tasks of all these tools will be changed. All of them will change. Our current building is aging and though it contains rich memories, it can no longer be renovated. An architect is now at work designing a new building in which our church will meet for worship and ministry. There is a serious leak in the bellows of our organ. As with the building that surrounds it, we must ask, "Can our organ be repaired?" And the even tougher question, "Should it be repaired?"

There are countless faith stories carried in the memory banks of believers. Many of these stories play back to the soundtrack of an organ. What should our churches do at this time of change? I do not have an easy answer. I do know that it is a time for respect, love and prayer—for rejoicing with those who rejoice and grieving with those who grieve.

On the other side of all these changes, when our grieving is finally done, we will still have each other, and we will still have the Lord. And he will have us. And I believe that there will come a day that my high school friend Tony will plug in his guitar, and my Iowa friend Bev will slide onto the organ bench, and we will sing a new song. And it will sound like heaven.

Sunday Morning Is a Story

Boredom is a preview of death, if not itself a form of death, and when trapped in prolonged boredom, even the most saintly of us will hope for, pray for, or even engineer relief, however demonic. Sincere Sunday worshipers will confess to welcoming in muffled celebration any interruption of the funeral droning. Be honest: Have you ever quietly cheered when a child fell off a pew, a bird flew in a window, the lights went out, the organ wheezed, the sound system picked up police calls, or a dog came down the aisle and curled up to sleep below the pulpit?

— Fred Craddock
Craddock Stories

My first feeling on Sunday morning is loneliness. Maybe this feeling is a residue from years of being one of the first people in town out of bed on Sunday. It is still dark out, and I am already tying my tie. I am putting on my most uncomfortable shoes, and I am thinking, "I'd like to be leading worship in southern California in one of those airy churches where you can wear Hawaiian shirts, shorts and flip-flops." I tiptoe past my sleeping family and go downstairs.

I am not hungry yet, but I pause in the kitchen long enough to make a cup of coffee. I hold it out away from me as I walk to the church building, hoping not to spill it and hoping to get there before the janitor. It is stupid, I know, but I do not want him to see me walking into the worship center with my coffee and give me that look that speaks volumes (although it is probably just my imagination). He has never once said anything to me about my coffee. Nobody has ever said anything to me about my coffee, but I am remembering the time there was an announcement in the church bulletin, "The deacons have respectfully requested that no coffee or red Kool-Aid be brought into the church sanctuary." I stopped bringing coffee for a while, and then one day, I watched a little boy after church regurgitate his red punch onto the carpet. That stain is still there. I figured the spell had been broken, and I went back to bringing my coffee.

I wander around turning on lights and adjusting equipment. The janitor arrives and gives me a good morning smile that I sometimes translate as "the look." I have learned to enjoy the role he plays in my morning, but it took me a while. It was over fifteen years ago that I was hired as worship leader, and the day I started was the day that the confusion over turf began. I was the church's first "worship leader." Prior to that, there was a well-established dance between the pastor, the organist, and the janitor. Since organists and janitors usually outlast pastors, they keep their routine in between pastorates, and new pastors drop into that routine. When I dropped in, no one knew what to do with this new puzzle piece called "worship leader." It took years.

The gang is all here, and we rehearse. After an hour, the first of the congregation starts filtering into the space. The loneliness gets pushed aside by other feelings vacillating between hope and fear—hope that God's people will rejoice in his presence and fear that I will do something as a leader to mess things up.

I am not the worship leader at our church any more. I do not have to get up so early. Why do I still feel lonely? I walk over to the building with my family. I wonder if anyone else feels lonely at the beginning of Sunday morning. Maybe it is a common feeling. Maybe others also ask "Who will I see first? Will they be glad to see me? Will they give me 'the look'?" Such feelings join all sorts of other feelings that are human and normal on a Sunday morning. It is every church member's opportunity to help each other take off their coats of loneliness, or shame, or superiority, or malaise and come together into God's presence bones out.

FOR LEADERS
OF STORYTELLERS

Who Do You
Suppose You Are?

As one called to teach women and men to preach, I am keenly concerned with how they conceive of themselves when they stand before the gathered faithful. In this regard I am reminded regularly of the painful and unrelenting question my mother used to ask me when I would do any one of a number of annoying childish things. Whether I had pulled my sister's hair, left my bicycle in the driveway, or interrupted an adult mid-sentence in a table conversation her question was swift and sure, "Just who do you think you are?" Although I didn't know it then, and I am quite sure she did not either, my mother was providing me with an early lesson in homiletics.
— Tim Brown
Perspectives, May, 2002

Host. It can be a verb meaning "to entertain." It can be a noun meaning "a crowd." It can refer to the bread in the Lord's Supper.

One summer, my parents asked several family friends to host their eight children while they took a much-needed vacation by themselves. I went with Grace McDowell, my Sunday School teacher who lived on a farm. I do not know how old she was, but I remember her gray hair. I was probably about ten years old. I remember her house as simple, quiet and clean. I do not remember what she fed me or where I slept, but I remember liking it there. I did not miss my parents much. I must have felt at home. She was a good host.

One day Grace said to me, "Jeff, you should go to college. Don't let anything stand in the way of that. Don't let money stand in the way." Why did she say that? Maybe Grace understood that I was missing something. No one in my family had ever been to college. Not my parents or grandparents. Grace saw some opportunity in my future, and she spoke potential into me. Was she intentionally forming in me value, courage and determination? Was she feeding not only my body but my spirit? What sort of host was she? I remember so little of my time spent at Grace's, but I remember that one thing she said to me.

I did go to college. I had no money. My parents had no money. They said, "Do what you like, it's yours to pay for." So I applied for financial aid, and suddenly I was in college followed by graduate school, with Grace's words accompanying me.

I remember the last time that I saw her. I came home on break from college one Christmas, and my mother suggested I go and visit Grace in the nursing home. I went. She barely acknowledged my presence. She said "Hello there," and shortly after that she asked me to leave. She said the devil was about to attack and she needed the time to pray. Whether or not she was out of her mind, she was no longer capable of being a good host. (My eighty-three-year-old friend Arlene says that maybe the spiritual battle is more real in that season of life.)

Host. It is the word that Tim Brown speaks into his preaching students, "Who do you suppose you are, preacher?" he asks them. He urges them to consider the word "host" in a gentle intertwining of at least two meanings of that word. They are ones who welcome others, and they are ones who feed the spirit. They are little hosts serving under the great host Jesus—Jesus the welcomer and Jesus the bread.

We theatre people should also answer Tim's question, "Who do you suppose you are?" whether we are serving in the theatre building or the church building. If we answer, "We're entertainers," that will be fine because "to host" and "to entertain" can be synonymous, another point at which theatre artists and leaders of worship intersect. We theatre artists of the body of Christ should say, "We are the little hosts assigned to the theatre. The one who made us and gifted us is the great host, the Lord of the theatre." The Lord of the theatre is Jesus who welcomes and feeds.

My college students sometimes arrive from high school with a dream of "making it big." Their definition of "entertainer" is not always "host." That other meaning of "entertainer" points a spotlight on fame rather than service. Such entertainers have forgotten who they are, and such forgetfulness has turned the word "entertainer" into a dirty word for the church.

My Christian college theatre colleagues and I are attempting to reclaim "entertainment." We woo our young artists to consider another way, where an entertainer is the host of a feast for the body and also for the spirit. We attempt to serve our audiences with joy, beauty and healing truth. When we entertain audience members, we invite them into our theatrical home. My fellow entertainers and I offer our audiences something that we have prepared for them, to help them live as they were intended. We provide sustenance for life's journey. We do our guests the service of providing a space for them to laugh and cry, to feel and reflect deeply. If we the hosts—the entertainers—do our jobs well, our guests respond with a deep sense of gratitude for their lives. Their applause says that they are grateful, not only to those entertainers who have served them, but to Someone else. Even if that Someone is not yet someone they know, they have begun to encounter him in beauty and truth. These audience members are like Joe Banks in the film *Joe vs. the Volcano* alone on his raft looking at the moon rising over the horizon and saying,

> *Dear God, whose name I do not know, thank you for my life. I forgot how big—thank you—thank you for my life.*

This experience is available to everyone who experiences beauty. As Paul says in his letter to the Romans,

> *Ever since the creation of the world his eternal power and divine nature, invisible though they are, have been understood and seen through the things he has made.*

Many years ago, I happened upon an audio recording by a Professor Rizzo. This was a vinyl recording with a lecture on it. It was not my recording, and I do not have a copy, but I remember listening to it. Rizzo was a theatre professor. I have forgotten where he taught, but I have not forgotten what he said. He said, "Great theatre makes the unseen seeable." Makes the unseen seeable. Whew.

If I am an effective entertainer host, I can help my audience see the otherwise invisible. And effective worship leader hosts do the same—help the unseen become seeable. Reality comes into focus. The mundane is set aside as the scales fall from our eyes. We are at a show! Truth and beauty aid clarity of sight. And in that moment of seeing, worship becomes the most natural response there is.

My mother and father once went to an estate sale and purchased a small oak desk. It had belonged to Grace McDowell. It was in her house that summer when I was ten. My parents had it refinished and gave it to Karen and me the day we were married. Today it sits in the corner of our living room, a reminder of that saintly woman who hosted me so well. It is a reminder too of another kind of host—the one mentioned in Hebrews 12, of which Grace is now surely a member.

> *Therefore, since we are surrounded by so great a cloud of witnesses, let us also lay aside every weight and sin which clings so closely, and let us run with perseverance the race that is set before us, looking to Jesus the pioneer and perfecter of our faith.... (1–2a, RSV)*

Passion

*Sadly, many of us take worship for granted. Worse, we craft it
around human agendas that often have nothing to do with
the divine activity of meeting and honoring God.*
— Sally Morgenthaler
Worship Evangelism

Our pastor took a new church. We found an interim pastor
named Don. Don had recently moved to our town after
retiring from a solid, stable church in suburban Chicago. Now
he was like a horse with no reins. He wanted to gallop as fast
and hard as he could for the rest of his life.

I was our church's worship leader, and Don invited me to
run with him. We met each Monday evening in his kitchen. His
wife set out coffee and treats, and off we went for a couple of
hours. We talked about the previous Sunday, and we talked
about the upcoming Sunday. But mostly, Don ran free, glowing
with passion about the importance of the church's mission and
the relationship of worship to that mission.

One day, Don showed up at my front door proclaiming,
"This is it! This is going to be our guidebook." He handed me a
copy of Sally Morgenthaler's *Worship Evangelism* which was
then hot off the press. So we studied it as much as our weekly
schedule allowed. It was a great year.

When we finally announced that we had called a new pastor, I phoned Don and asked if he was going to stay at our church. He said, "I'll come over and we'll talk about it."

Don arrived and sat at our dining room table. I had asked Karen to join us, because I had a sense of what was coming, and I wanted her help. Don was pretty somber for a change. "I'm not sure I can stay," he said. "I'm not certain that enough people in this church are serious about worship." I told him that I did not know if his assessment was correct, but I told him that I was serious. Karen said that she, too, was serious. "There," I said, "there are at least three of us. And what about our new pastor. You believe he's serious, don't you?"

"I'm not sure that's enough," Don said.

Don had been in our denomination for a long time. He had studied in a denomination college and seminary. He knew the denomination's theology of worship. He knew that each new liturgical guide that the denomination had published during his ministry had affirmed this empowering and freeing paragraph from its 1793 constitution:

> *Her Mode of Worship is expressed in the Liturgy, where forms of several prayers are given, without any idea, however, of restraining her members to any particular terms or fixed standards for prayer. Firmly believing that the gifts of the Holy Spirit for the edification of Zion in every age are promised and bestowed . . .*

These words were potent, and Don believed them. He wanted to know how the gifts of the Holy Spirit for the edification of Zion were being bestowed in this local church at this time. What would guide the worshipers of this church? Would they access the gifts of the Spirit or would they lean too heavily upon pattern? Don was looking to join a people who wanted to raise their sails to the wind of the Spirit. He did not want to sit in the harbor. My friend Arlene remembers a poster she saw when she worked in Zambia. It contained a popular saying that is probably attributable to Rear Admiral Grace Murray Hopper, also known as "Amazing Grace Hopper":

> *A ship in the harbor is safe, but that's not what ships are made for.*

Don wanted to be moving with every day he had left.

"Give me a chance to write something down," I said. "If you can get behind it, then we can go to work together." Don agreed.

With the help of the worship planning team, I did write something down, which we printed into bookmarks to give to the whole church. See what you think.

> *Worship, says David Mains, is most often understood in scripture to mean "paying God a compliment." Warren Wiersbe points us to the Greek word used in the scripture:* proskuneo. *Literal sources for that word include "to kneel" or "to kiss toward," like a child blowing kisses to his or her parent, after that same parent taught them how to blow kisses by blowing kisses toward the child first.*
>
> *How are the above definitions made observable in our worship?*
>
> *Here are some suggested guides. Anyone observing worship should hear, see, and feel us affirming the following:*

1. We expect God to reveal his presence.
"*Where two or three come together in my name, there am I with them.*" (Matthew 18:20)

2. We delightedly, passionately revere God's Word.
"*How sweet are Thy words to my taste, sweeter than honey to my mouth! I gain understanding from Thy precepts; therefore I hate every wrong path. Thy word is a lamp unto my feet and a light unto my path.*" (Psalm 119:103–105, NIV/KJV)

3. We welcome others into God's presence—those who already know him as beloved Lord and friend, and also those who are wondering whether he could be.
Jesus spoke the following words to a Samaritan woman who was not living a Godly life. He offered her living water and delivered to her one of the Bible's great statements about the meaning and importance of worship: "A time is coming and has now come when the true worshipers will worship the Father in spirit and truth. They are the kind of worshipers the Father seeks." (John 4:23, NIV *adapted*)

4. We affirm that we are not here because of what we get but because God has already given so much that we want to express our love to him in return.
"*How great is the love the Father has lavished on us, that we should be called children of God! And that is what we are!*" (1 John 3:1a)

5. We affirm that God is active in this church, and his presence excites us!
"*The* LORD *will guide you always; he will satisfy*

*your needs in a sun-scorched land. He will
strengthen your frame. You will be like a well-wa-
tered garden...."* (Isaiah 58:11)

6. We believe in prayer's power!
*"Pray for each other that you may be healed. The
prayer of a righteous person is powerful and effective."* (James 5:16, NIV *adapted*)

**7. We celebrate God, and we are also humbled
before his greatness and mystery.**
*"The twenty-four elders fall down before him who
sits on the throne, and worship him who lives for
ever and ever. They lay their crowns before the
throne...."* (Revelation 4:10)

8. We love one another.
*"A new commandment, I give you: Love one an-
other. As I have loved you, so you must love one another. By this all people will know that you are my
disciples, if you love one another."* (John 13:34–35,
NIV *adapted*)

Soon after our new pastor was installed, Don and his wife
Audrey became members of our church. Audrey recently fell
and broke her leg, and Don's failing eyesight keeps him from
driving or preaching, but with their faces, voices, hands and spirits, they are going steady for the goal, passions burning bright.

The Source of Creativity

*When, a few years later, I stumbled across that Benedictine
monastery, I found worship that was far more accessible and
refreshing. The monks, it seemed, were in less of a hurry, less
frantic to fill the air with a quantity of words.*
— Kathleen Norris
Amazing Grace

How does one keep on being creative?" Three senior seminary students were sitting in the backyard of our rented
cottage on Lake Michigan. They had given up their Saturday
night to be with Karen and me. They had invited themselves.
We were honored that they cared to nose around in the clut-
tered storeroom of our experience. And the first question of the
night was, "How does one keep on being creative?"

I suddenly felt childish. What contribution could I make
in the face of such a mystery? How often had I not wondered
this very thing myself? Although I may have grown creative in
the past, the latest ripe apple picked from that tree was the last
one there. And if I could manage to find another apple, that one
would surely be the last. I never had a promise that the tree
would bear more fruit. I expected that Karen felt the same. I expected that all of us sat there feeling the same unspoken fear.

I glanced toward the west. I stared. Something had happened while I was not looking. A gray wash of clouds had blown

in from the Chicago side of the lake. The sun had settled just below the horizon, leaving only reflected light behind. The clouds, the light and the water were a seamless image. The horizon was gone. It was gone. The clouds washed up on our shore. The lake swept up and away over our heads. I knew this water had so many personalities, but this was new. For a while, I was gone. How long? A heartbeat? A couple of years? I forgot the company and the conversation. I saw the sky. It was eternity.

What is the correct answer to the seminary students' first question? What would you have said? I wish you had been there.

Three days later, I was back in Chicago. I went to the Garfield Conservatory to see the Chihuly blown glass exhibit. It was amazing. The plants and trees were more amazing still. Hundreds, huge and tiny. One plant had little leaves that folded together into the shape of a small shrimp, and when fully mature, a little, colorful shrimp's tail appears. Dale Chihuly had been inspired by a visit to this world class conservatory. His strange glass shapes now nestled among God's own weird and wonderful creations.

Out a side door, I turned the corner and there was a gravel path that circled around and around seven times. A small sign told me it was a labyrinth. A labyrinth is different than a maze. There is no puzzle in the path itself. The path simply folds around on itself, leading to a center point. The traveler is invited to walk in, pause, and walk out. It is, historically, a spiritual activity. The investment is time, and the product is unknown. I took the bait. I walked slowly. A couple joined me on the path. They chattered the whole time, laughing and enjoying one another. When they got to the center, they giggled, cut across the grass and disappeared. I made it to the center, paused, and headed back out the way I had come in. I walked past a river birch that stood by the outer ring. There were birch trees in my yard when I was growing up. I used to mow around them. They are eccentric trees that reignite my childhood memories, so I am always on the lookout for them. I had not seen this river birch on the way in, but now it was there. Where had it come from? I continued to loop around and around. I decided to pause on the path and look around while standing still. Perhaps there would be another river birch I had not noticed. I looked up. Suddenly there was a hummingbird feeding among the tall orange flowers not ten feet away. I had never before seen a humming bird so close and for so long. I stood there for several minutes. His back was green and shining. I continued down the path. On the last loop around, I saw a dainty fountain hidden among the flowers across from the labyrinth. It was obvious. How had I missed it?

I do not know the answer to the seminary students' question. I suppose there are answers, but I do not know them. There are people who teach creativity theory, but I do not. All I know is how it seems to work out for me. I pause on the path. I look around. I wait.

So many times, creative activity ("creativity") is simply picking beauties from God's garden.

Fresh Understanding

*But we must take care—as I have elsewhere explained—lest
the people sing only with their lips, like sounding pipes or harps
and without understanding.*
— Martin Luther

We arrived home after being away for five months. We
walked into depression. The paint on the side of the
house was suddenly peeling. There was mildew on the bath-
room ceiling. A kitchen cabinet door hung from one hinge. The
flaws leapt out at us. The truth is that all these things were present when we left, but we had grown accustomed to them. Now
we saw them with newcomer eyes. We vowed to walk through
the house and make a list, taking advantage of this fresh perspective before we got calloused again.

We arrived at church on our first Sunday back wearing our
newcomer glasses. I made a list, given my renewed perspective.
Here it is—the list of some of the peeling paint on worship at
my church. Stay with me. This adventure will not all be negative.
By the end, I will have shared some of the joys of coming home.

The sign out front is old fashioned and rusty. The spot-
lights in the sanctuary spill everywhere, no focus whatsoever.
There is a hum in the sound system. There is a hiss from a leak
in the organ bellows. The microphones hanging over the choir
are actually body mics and there is about twenty feet of extra

cable all wound up into a ball, hanging like the back room at Radio Shack. The carpet is twenty years out of fashion and there is a bare spot on the platform carpet where the old choir rail used to sit. The pulpit does not match the rest of the platform furniture, and it is too low for our current pastor. There is a pile of cable stacked on top of a cabinet at the back of the choir loft, visible to half of the congregation.

The service begins. The pastor's body microphone has a worn spot on the transmitter and the mic itself is still held to his tie with a clip that broke about seven years ago. The excess cable hangs loosely in front of his pants, and I am suddenly reminded that we no longer have a worship leadership team in our organizational structure here. Consequently there is no protective critique system which empowers someone to say, "Oh, and by the way, Pastor, your mic cable needs to be tucked out of the way so that it doesn't dangle in the front of your pants."

The four songs chosen include one classic hymn and three more contemporary hymns. I remember how much I once learned by asking some of our elder saints to share with me the titles of ten of their favorite hymns. Today I wonder how much we would learn if we asked our members what song styles they listen to day by day and what church songs they associate with some of the significant memories of their lives.

The drums play all the way through each and every song, leveling out all potential builds and mood shifts. Even with drum support, tempos change awkwardly within songs and between instruments, reminding me that the monitor system in this sanctuary is inadequate for musicians to actually hear one another and stay together.

Downbeats are provided by a capable leader, but her cueing is not supported by the instrumentalists, the choir or the lyrics on the screen. What I mean is that the instruments should

help us feel secure, leading us into the next stanza or song. There
should be musical preparation—provision of "Ready, set" as
well as "go." Likewise the choir should know the cueing and
their faces and voices should suggest security rather than hesi-
tancy. The lyrics on screen (and the ways they transition) should
clarify whether we will sing another refrain or fall silent. Hesi-
tancy at these moments of transition suggests insecurity in leadership, which easily spreads insecurity all around the room.

There is more. On this Sunday we are installing the elders
and deacons. They are asked to respond, "Yes, truly with all my
heart." They are not certain of their words and do not want to
be embarrassed, so their responses sound like the trailed-off
dronings of school children at their recitations: "Yes, troophy-
ifellimart. . . ." These are our leaders, and they need rehearsal so
they can respond with passion, driving through to the phrase
"ALL MY HEART!" For that matter, we as a congregation
could use some rehearsing ourselves so we read responsively
with some actual responsiveness and joy. If I were a true newcomer, I would guess that these people did not much care for
their religion.

The pastor reads the questions for the leaders from a page
he has taken out of the big red plastic three-ring binder notebook that the denomination sends out. Not using the entire garish notebook is a step in the right direction, but we should
provide a leather binding for such important documents, unless
they are going to be committed to memory, which, of course,
would be wonderful.

The choir is too small and sings with less precision than
they are able. They are not embarrassing. Neither do they thrill.

The communion plates are brought to the choir members
just as they are about to start singing.

A soloist sings during the passing of the cup. He finishes

before the cup is completely passed, and silence falls in the room. I am sitting down front, so I do not know precisely what is going on, but I can hear the clink of the plates being stacked at the back of the sanctuary. I suddenly realize that I have missed silence in the worship. We need silence. We need moments when we are together quiet before our God.

This worship was not bad. Its warts stood out to me on this newcomer day, but there is much to celebrate. I sense a spirit of peace and unity. The new greeter's program has stuck, and as we arrived, the door was swung open and a welcoming face beamed. The handshakes and hugs during the greeting time and after church are warm and sincere. There are fabulous resources of faith, prayer, and Bible scholarship. The budget is balanced, but we have a Spirit led pastor who consistently reminds us that church is far more than budget. He preaches to us with excellence, and he practices what he preaches.

The first cue of the morning is executed with precision, as the pastor overlaps his entrance perfectly with the end of the organ prelude. Such precision captures our attention and builds energy in the room. There is an ease and sense of humor about the place. An interview during the service helps us affirm our core spiritual values, and the laying on of hands during the installation service is genuinely moving. I am also especially moved by the simplicity of musical colors added on occasion (flute, saxophone). The soloist sings a song that is perfectly matched to the moment ("Surely we'll learn what grace is for as we sail to heaven's shore"), and he sings with security and honesty.

As we sing the closing Doxology, all the instruments fall silent. We are in the moment together in a room, no distractions, at worship. Perfect. This ... more of this ... will draw me back.

I am the last one in the room. I still hear that sound system hum. I track it to the synthesizer, which someone left on. I turn it off, but the hum remains. I stoop, following my ears, going to my knees. As I place my hands down, I realize the floor is vibrating. I go to the basement and sneak into the women's washroom. I turn off the lights and the fan. I go back upstairs, and the hum is gone. Next Sunday morning it will return. I wonder how long it will be before I do not hear it anymore.

In Search of Humility

Are any among you suffering? They should pray. Are any cheer-
ful? They should sing songs of praise. Are any among you sick?
They should call for the elders of the church and have them
pray over them, anointing them with oil in the name of the
Lord. The prayer of faith will save the sick, and the Lord will
raise them up; and anyone who has committed sins will be for-
given. Therefore confess your sins to one another, and pray for
one another, so that you may be healed. The prayer of the right-
eous is powerful and effective.

— James 5:13–16, NRSV

D o you have a place to humble yourself?" our pastor asked
us during the morning worship service. The question
touched a tender spot in my heart.

I first began seriously to ponder the role of personal and
specific confession in the Christian life when I read Richard
Foster's *Celebration of Discipline*. Reading that chapter sparked
in me a longing for a place to confess my sins. The Protestant
Reformation, while affirming the priesthood of every believer,
had somehow misplaced James's commendation that we confess
our sins to one another.

I stumbled in among Free Methodists during my college
years, so I learned about John Wesley's accountability groups. I
had never personally experienced a group that practices Wesleyan accountability, but when I later lived in Pennsylvania, I

was part of a Free Methodist church where some of the old timers told me they remembered when the weekly rhythm used to include "house groups" that met in homes each Wednesday evening. In accordance with part of Wesleyan practice, each person around the circle would answer the following questions every week:

1. *What sins have you committed since our last meeting?*
2. *What temptations have you faced?*
3. *How did you escape the temptations?*
4. *What have you thought, said, or done, that you are wondering whether or not it is a sin?*
5. *Is there something you do not wish to tell us?*

Now that is the real deal.

Hannah did a work trip with her youth group, renovating a school in Minneapolis. Their contact person at the school invited them to church on Sunday. During the worship service, the pastor said, "Who has a birthday in July?" Those with birthdays stood up, and the congregation sang to them. "Who has a wedding anniversary this month?" Those with anniversaries stood up, and the pastor asked how many years, and the congregation applauded for them. Then the pastor asked, "Is there anyone here who has stayed clean from an addiction for the past month?" Someone stood up. Then another. The best applause yet. That is tough. That is even tricky and dangerous. It could turn manipulative. But it seems real to me, and if that church were in my town, I would be worshiping there.

"Do you have a place to humble yourself?" our pastor asked. I knew my answer was no. He said, "We're starting accountability groups here this fall." I have been part of an accountability group a few times in my life. My experience is that they are very difficult to form. And they get sidetracked easily. I have longed for a group like Wesley's group. So I was eager to hear about these groups forming up at my church. "They're going to be formed of three people who are committed to meet an hour once a month," said the pastor. I was thinking, how can you stay accountable meeting only once a month? My friend, Dan, when he was freshly facing his alcoholism, needed to find an Alcoholics Anonymous meeting pretty much every day. If I met once a month with an accountability group, could I remember the sins I had committed since our last meeting? And would one hour be enough?

After worship, I helped clean up the communion dishes. As I was leaving the building, I saw the pastor alone at the front of the worship center. He started talking to me, and I thanked him for his sermon. I used the opportunity to ask him how those accountability groups would form. He said that someone from the group would call the church to tell who was in the group, and then there would be a meeting with all the groups to teach them what to do and how to report their progress. I asked him how the three people would be chosen. He told me someone would have to take the leadership. I said, "So someone has to call someone and say, 'Will you be in an accountability group with me?'" He nodded. I admitted that was the point at which I stumble. He said, "I've heard that same thing many times now." I said, "Well, I'll talk to you later. Have a good Sunday." He said, "You, too."

But the conversation was not over. It continued as I walked home alone from church:

EAGER JEFF
Why don't you ask somebody?

HESITANT JEFF

Like who? There's nobody.

EAGER JEFF

Well, what about asking our two pastors? That would make three.

HESITANT JEFF

I'd love to. But won't they have lots of people that would love to have them? It wouldn't be fair for me to take one of them let alone both of them. And besides, they're younger than me. They'll want someone their own age. Or maybe they don't want another church meeting to go to. Maybe they should be home with their families instead of helping me. Forget about the pastors.

EAGER JEFF

Pastors need accountability, too.

HESITANT JEFF

They're men of initiative. If they really wanted you, they would ask you. Leave them alone.

EAGER JEFF

What about Tom? He's your age. He's good-humored, humble, gracious, and you trust him.

HESITANT JEFF

Yes. He's a great idea. I bet other people will think of him, too. And he has cancer, so maybe now is not a good time. Maybe later.

EAGER JEFF

Okay, what about Dennis?

HESITANT JEFF

He doesn't attend our church.

EAGER JEFF

Okay, what about Ray?

HESITANT JEFF

He's too good of a Christian.

EAGER JEFF

You're right, forget him. What about. . . . I can't think of anyone else. Shall we go down the church directory?

HESITANT JEFF

Do I really want to be telling my sins to people that are not close enough friends that I can easily think of them?

EAGER JEFF

Well maybe the truth is you don't have friends.

HESITANT JEFF

Maybe not. Lots of acquaintances.
     (Pause.)
This is too hard. Let's change the subject.

EAGER JEFF

No. What is your problem? Really.

HESITANT JEFF

I dunno. I guess it's mostly that I don't want to be
stuck in a group with someone who said yes to me just
because they didn't want to offend me by telling me
they didn't really want to be in a group with me.

EAGER JEFF

That would be a bummer.

HESITANT JEFF

So, what do you think I should do?

There was a long pause. Then I got home and it was time for
lunch.

I do not know how, but I just did it. I did not finish the
internal argument, but I took one step. I asked Tom. He immediately said yes he would do it, no matter who else I asked. He
wanted to do it. Then I asked Dennis and even though he does
not go to my church and does not know Tom, he said yes.

We began to negotiate for a time, which took three or four
days. During those four days, Tom went to the doctor and was
told that he had two months to live. I saw him at church the following Sunday. He asked me what was happening about the accountability group. I said, "Do you still want to do it?" He said
yes, and I said, "Well, I'll talk to Dennis and see what we can
work out." He said, "Okay, but I'd like to get this group started
right away." I said I would call him soon, and I did. Dennis and
I met later that week at Tom's house. Tom was not there. His
wife told us he must have forgotten about us. He was having a
rare good day, so he had gone to see his son. "I'll call him and
see if he can come home," she said. We asked her not to. We
would see him later. And we did, but when we did, Tom had

taken a turn for the worse. He rested in his easy chair in his sweats. He answered the questions as best he could, and he dozed while we gave our answers.

We probably had a total of three meetings with Tom. We witnessed him maintaining the hope of heaven while staring death in the face. Then one meeting we showed up and nobody was home. Dennis and I stayed at the kitchen table and answered the questions and prayed. As we were leaving, Tom's youngest daughter pulled into the drive and told us they had taken him to the hospital. We went and teased him for not wanting to answer the questions. He smiled at us through a morphine haze. We sang a hymn and went out.

Tom died a few weeks later. It seemed like minutes. He and Dennis and I were accountability brothers until the end. It was the real deal.

Leaders Who Worship

Only by participating can we understand what it is Christians do in worship.

— James White
Documents of Christian Worship

I met Jeremy at a conference about ten years ago. I think he was in middle school, playing the piano for a middle school gospel choir. I remember that he did not seem to have any music and that he kept his eyes glued to the conductor. Amazing.

I just returned from a conference where I once again saw Jeremy. He must be out of college now, still playing the piano for a gospel choir. He played a solo and it was awesome. But what impressed me the most, more than his musical ability, was the fact that he was a worshiper. There was one moment during a choir song that the instruments dropped out for an *a cappella* verse. During that verse, I glanced over at Jeremy, buried there behind the piano at the side of the stage. He had his eyes glued to the conductor, while at the same time his hand was raised in worship. The moment the choir sang its final *a cappella* amen, the congregation was applauding, and so was Jeremy. He was supporting the conductor, the choir, the Lord, and us. Amazing.

Jeremy's story is the story that should be happening in front of every church. It is the story of the servants of worship who are never bystanders, always participants.

WORSHIP KNOWS
THE WHOLE STORY

Birth: One Pastor's Wife's Saturday

To worship God means to serve him. Basically there are two ways to do it. One way is to do things for him that he needs to have done—run errands for him, carry messages for him, fight on his side, feed his lambs, and so on. The other way is to do things for him that you need to do—sing songs for him, create beautiful things for him, give things up for him, tell him what's on your mind and in your heart, in general rejoice in him and make a fool of yourself for him the way lovers have always made fools of themselves for the one they love.

A Quaker Meeting, a Pontifical High Mass, the Family Service at First Presbyterian, a Holy Roller Happening—unless there is an element of joy and foolishness in the proceedings, the time would be better spent doing something useful.

— Frederick Buechner
Wishful Thinking: A Theological ABC

I was asked to speak to a group of pastors and their spouses. I simply called several of them on the phone and then wrote the following story for them based on actual incidents they shared with me. They seemed to enjoy being able to laugh at as well as celebrate these events that were—for them—both unique and common. You could say that what follows is a true story, except that these events did not all happen to the same person. They could not have. Could they?

It was a Saturday morning. She was pregnant, expecting their third child. She had spent the morning feeling some contractions. At high noon, she could tell that this was it—high noon in more ways than one. She said to her husband, "Honey, it's time to go to the hospital." The trouble was that her husband was a pastor. And he had a wedding that afternoon.

At this moment it seemed to her that her entire married life had been a tug of war between her needs and the needs of the church. Even simple needs, like ketchup. Since they lived in a parsonage right next to the church building, whenever there was a church dinner and the church refrigerator ran out of ketchup, one of the hospitality committee would turn to her and say, "Do you happen to have a bottle of ketchup we could use?"

Yes, she did. She would go get it. It would get used up during the evening. The money would come out of her personal budget. Over the years this event would repeat itself, and it added up. Ketchup. Mustard. Relish. Butter. Salad dressing. Milk. Coffee. Such little things, but it was at moments of stress that the little things spoke to her and said, "Only the church matters."

This message, "Only the church matters," was first whispered to her when her fiancé (now husband) was in seminary. He had a little student pastorate. His responsibility was simply to show up and preach every weekend. One Sunday, shortly after they had started dating, she went along for the first time to his church. While he prepared the sanctuary, she stood in the narthex. Several of the parishioners also stood there looking at her. Finally one of them said,

"Are you going to sing?"

"No. I don't sing."

"Do you play the piano?"

"No. I don't play the piano."

Silence. That was it. The silence asked why she was there. She knew her real answer was that, "She was there for him, she didn't want to be here, she didn't like it here, she wouldn't be here unless he were here." And immediately she had felt guilty for feeling this way, so selfish. So she unconsciously pressed down her own needs, even then, and told herself, "The church, that's what matters. Only the church."

She did not know it, but deep inside, she had risen to the challenge—the challenge of trying to win the church over, and thereby proving something—something having to do with her own worth. Like the time that she made a Thanksgiving meal for the entire congregation. Granted, it was a small congregation, but the money for the food had come out of her own pocket.

At the end of the meal, one lady who had stayed to clean up off-handedly commented, "That's an awful lot of leftover potatoes—waste of money."

Well, this was true, but she had wanted to shout back, "It's not the church's money, it's my money, and if I want to waste three dollars' worth of potatoes, I'll waste three dollars' worth of potatoes!"

Her inner voice whispered that the affirmation she craved did not matter. Only the church mattered.

That inner voice was hovering close by on this Saturday noon when she desperately needed to go to the hospital and none of the church people who had said they would take care of the other two children when the time came could be reached now that the time had come.

Her husband continued to make preparations to go to the wedding.

Not to worry. They finally found someone who would take the kids, and at 1:00 they pulled up to the hospital, and he, with the weight of the responsibility of his parish upon him, dropped off his wife with the promise to return as soon as possible. She walked through the hospital doors alone.

Ah, the lonely road. For her, this was the road much traveled. It started every Saturday night when he closed the study door to put the finishing touches on the next day's sermon. Sunday morning, he left early to prepare for the service. She got the kids up and dressed and breakfasted and to church. She had lost track of the number of times her kindergarten son had made his Sunday morning pronouncement, "I hate church!" And as an afterthought, "And I hate Sunday school too."

She sat as a single mother wrestling her children during the service. All the other children seemed to be perfect angels.

After Sunday dinner, which she prepared, her husband took a much-needed nap. When he got up, he put the finishing touches on his evening sermon, grabbed a sandwich standing up, and left early to prepare for the service. She got the kids dressed and suppered and to church, with her son saying all the while, "I hate church. Why do we have to go on Sunday nights? The other kids don't have to go."

He was right. The other kids weren't there. It was a vicious cycle. Since the Sunday evening crowd was mostly older folks, the service was tailored to their tastes. Thus it was even more unpalatable to her children, making them especially restless. For her, Sunday night was more like professional wrestling than worship.

But she had tried staying home one Sunday night. The next Sunday night, an upstanding elder saint had commented, "It's nice to see the Pastor's wife in church." So she went.

The rest of the week was equally lonely. Her husband

kept office hours during the day, did calling in the late afternoons and met with committees in the evenings. When he was home, he would observe, "You don't want me home for me. You just want a babysitter." It was true. She was getting so that she couldn't stand to look at the kids.

She knew that her husband was under pressure to keep the parishioners from saying, "He's not working hard enough." So, she tried to do her part, but she was starting to feel like the wicked witch saying, "Get home!" How many times had she asked herself, "Is there something wrong with me? Don't I love God enough?"

Yes, she did love God. She loved him desperately, longingly.

In my life, Lord, be glorified, be glorified.

A snatch of a worship chorus floated through her mind as she walked down the hospital corridor alone.

In my life, Lord, be glorified today.

She pulled herself together and signed in, between contractions. She settled into a comfortable birthing room. Things began to brighten a bit.

She was in good hands. One day, they would look back at this and laugh. Like the time when they were first married and she was still in her professional mode. She had gone away on a consulting job, and her husband had made his own pink Jell-O salad to take to the church potluck. He had doubled the recipe but forgot to double the water. For years after that, whenever someone brought pink Jell-O salad to a potluck, everyone laughingly referred to it as "Pastor's Plaster."

And there was the time one of their parishioners got arrested for bouncing a check, and they had to go down and bail her out. It was their church treasurer.

Or the time an especially cultured woman had visited their church, and their little girl had looked at the woman and made a face like—well, if you'd really like to know, stand in front of the mirror, put your thumbs in the corners of your mouth, your index fingers in the outside corners of your eyes, squeeze together, and then put your little fingers in your nostrils and lift!

These were things to laugh about. "A merry heart does good, like a medicine."

Another contraction . . . and she suddenly felt so tired. Tired and alone.

She was tired of having to cover for people who did not do their jobs in nursery, Sunday school, cleaning, getting special music, etc.

She was tired of feeling responsible at every Bible study whether she was the appointed leader or not.

She was tired of people complaining to her in hopes that it would get to the pastor.

She was tired of the annual salary evaluations.

She was tired of always having to say, "I got it on sale," for fear that people would say they were getting paid too much.

She was tired of not being able to share her true prayer requests.

She was tired and alone and empty. She imagined walking into worship and saying, "I'm not smiling any more. In fact, I'm giving up my faith today. You have faith for me."

In my life, Lord, be glorified, be glorified.

She picked up the phone and called the church building. Her husband answered.

"How much longer? Is the wedding over?"

"No, it hasn't even started."

"Please hurry."

"Is the baby coming?!"

"No. But I need you."

"I know. I'll be there as soon as I possibly can."

She hung up the phone.

In this room, Lord, be glorified today.

The minutes and contractions ticked by. The nurses were there. But no beloved soul mate to walk through the dark valley. The doctors came and went. Each time the door opened, her heart leapt in anticipation. Which was worse—the contractions or the opening and closing of the door? She recalled the proverb, "Hope deferred makes the heart sick."

She was close now. So close. The anesthesiologist arrived to prepare her for a spinal. It was a new procedure to her. She hadn't had it with the first two children. Had she made the right choice? Were the medical risks too great?

Fear began to creep in like the ex-con who had strolled up to their parsonage late one night while her husband was away. It was their second church. An inner city pastorate. She was alone that night. Alone with their newborn baby. A knock at the door. She opened it and recognized him immediately: he was the husband half of one of the many couples they had invited to their home over the past months. The man whose battered wife had later come to them. They had counseled the woman to seek help and shelter and safety. Could this man have found out? Was he now seeking revenge?

"Do you know where my wife is?"

"Yes."

"Can you tell me?"

"She has moved to another city."

For some reason the man turned and walked away. She did not know why. But that night she had learned what it meant to taste fear. It was a startling bitterness on the tongue.

And now here she was, dining at fear's table again. She knew that Christians are supposed to be victorious over fear. Did this mean that Christians did not even feel fear? No.

In this fear, Lord, be glorified, be glorified.

She had gradually learned that she could not confront human trauma with an institutionalized God. Like the time she had gone to visit the grieving mother whose suicidal daughter was placed in a psychiatric hospital and then stabbed to death by a fellow inmate. She had remained speechless in the presence of that heartsick mother. Listening. Learning.

Now, with no one to speak words of comfort to her, a time when perhaps even Job's comforters would have been better than nothing, she was silent before the Lord. And oddly, or perhaps it wasn't so odd, she remembered the weekend a half a year ago when they had brought in a Lay Witness Mission to their church. At the end of the weekend, there was an invitation to recommitment. She and her husband had walked forward and knelt to pray, recommitting their lives to Christ. A few minutes later, she opened her eyes and peeked around to see their seven-year-old daughter kneeling just behind them. And she looked beyond her daughter and saw that the center aisle of the church building was lined with kneeling people.

So many people want to have strong faith—to live completely for Jesus—if only they have someone to show them the way. "How beautiful upon the mountains are the feet of the one who brings good news."

The spinal was finished. Pain now gone, she found herself alone with her God.

In this new birth, be glorified today.

The door to the hospital room swung gently open. It was her husband. Never in the history of ministry had a pastoral call been so welcome.

A flood of such welcomings came rushing to her mind. Like the time her husband had rifled her basket collection to make Easter baskets for a needy family—and upon discovering that he had given away a basket that had great sentimental value to her, he had gone and purchased brand new larger baskets and filled them and somehow managed a trade. He had been a welcome sight as he came up the front walk, bringing her lost basket home.

A welcoming like the young woman she had shared room mother duties with at the grade school. A woman who wasn't interested in "religion" as she called it. They had many good talks, but she had never even invited the woman to church. She knew this young woman would say, "Back off!" Then one Sunday morning, this woman came into the church building bringing her daughters. After worship, this very same hardened-against-God woman came to the back with tear-stained cheeks—and it wasn't a pastor's wife who led her to the Lord. It was one room mother welcoming another room mother into the heavenly family.

And finally, this Saturday's joy foretold for her the final welcoming, when her elder brother, Jesus, would run to greet her on heavenly streets and shout to all around, "Hey everybody, this is my sister that I've been telling you about. Welcome home, sis."

And suddenly, before she knew it, it was over. The doctor was handing her husband the scissors to cut the umbilical cord.

Here was a wonder.

Another child whom she would try to keep quiet on Sunday nights by secretly nursing him under a blanket the older two children would suddenly want to play tug of war with.

Another child who would think he had thirty-six grandmas because of the way the church ladies would spoil him.

Another child who would lurk around corners in the parsonage, eavesdropping on adult conversations, discovering ecclesiology, sampling theology, and catching faith. That night when her husband leaned over the hospital bed rail and kissed her goodnight, she loved him with all her heart. She knew he did not love her as Christ loved the church. That was too high a standard. She forgave him for being human. She knew he forgave her, for he also had suffered, and forgiveness is willingness to accept suffering that you did not deserve. On this Saturday night, she knew they would both continue to forgive these people who mattered—for whom they would give their ketchup and their lives.

She heard him steal quietly from the room. She knew where he was headed. To his study to put the finishing touches on his sermon for the next morning.

Sex: Judy's Terrible Wonderful Afternoon

> *The beauty and order of nature are not gratuitous. The tapestry does not exist for its own sake, just to be admired. Its grit and grandeur has a purpose. The prettiness has a point. Nature is, as Psalm 19 says in the King James Version, God's "handiwork." It has God's fingerprints all over it. John Calvin called creation "the theater of God's glory." It is a place where, and a way that, God performs.*
>
> — Nathan Bierma
> *Bringing Heaven Down to Earth*

A dear friend of ours stopped by. I will call her Judy. She said, "Want to hear about my day yesterday?" We said yes, and she warned us that she was still tired and weepy, so she might not do very well. Then she plunged ahead.

Judy had driven to meet her son and his girlfriend. Her son was transferring colleges, and his girlfriend, who had recently graduated from college, was also planning to find an apartment in this new college town.

Together the three of them toured the campus. They stopped at the housing office and learned it was campus policy for students who were not yet seniors to live on campus. The son's face fell. They stepped outside the office carrying a housing application to complete. The young man told his mother he was about to cause great disappointment to two other guys who were hoping to live together with him and his girlfriend in a rented house near campus—in fact, they already had a house on hold with a realtor. This arrangement was new to Judy. She bit her tongue, aware that her relationship with her son was at that universally dangerous moment of passage from childhood into adulthood. While her son was considering what to do, she suggested that they stop and say hello to a friend of their family: the college president.

The president was in his office, and he greeted them with warmth, rejoicing that Judy's son would be attending his college. "Are you here looking for an apartment?" asked the president. Judy explained that they had just discovered the housing policy. The president said, "Well, we have a lot more men than usual attending this fall, maybe there's room for an exception to the housing policy." Judy told him no, that they had not come there to secure his intervention. When they left, she gave the president a hug and again told him that she was not expecting him to intervene regarding the housing. Outside the president's office, the girlfriend said, "What a wonderful man. He's the kind of person that you wouldn't ever want to do anything to disappoint."

Judy took a breath and asked her son and his girlfriend if she could treat them to a late lunch. "Pick a place that you couldn't otherwise afford," she said. They chose a lovely Italian bistro in the center of town. After they had ordered, Judy said, "We need to talk about the elephant in the room." She paused. Then she said, "Are you two sexually active?" Without looking at one another, the two young people immediately told the truth. Yes.

Judy did not tell us all the details of the next two hours. What she told us was that the young woman cried through most of it. And so did Judy. Judy told them, "Sex is not something that is just yours. It happens in the context of your life in a community and what you do as a sexual couple impacts the community." Ultimately, Judy's son made her proud with his own tears and respectfulness. "I don't want to disappoint you," he said. "And I don't want to set a bad example."

But make no mistake. It was not easy, and it was not neat, and it was not done by the end of two hours. Her son argued sex was natural, a part of a healthy relationship. His girlfriend admitted her parents did not know and would be very disappointed if they ever found out.

I asked if this all happened at the restaurant. Yep, said Judy, waiters were stopping by with their usual questions, "How is everything? Anything I can get you?" Judy said their food was great, and they even ate some of it. Outside the restaurant, Judy looked them each in the eye and told them she loved them. And she left. Her son was on his own.

Judy was supposed to meet another young couple who lived in that town. She was late, but she called and asked if she could still come over. When she got there, her friends could tell she had been crying. They led her into the dining room where there were places set, and there was fruit cut and laid out in the middle of the table. "Oh, I'm so sorry," said Judy, "You're expecting guests." The wife of the young couple laughed and said, "We're expecting you."

For the next hour Judy gently revealed her mother's heart to this younger couple who did not yet have children. They listened. She was struck that they told her she was very unusual. This conversation was not the sort of thing about which parents usually talk with their children. "Yes, but I don't know if I've done the right thing," sobbed Judy.

"You're doing it," said the young husband. He reminded

Judy that her son would never forget this day. He said, "Now if your son and his girlfriend have sex again, his mother will be in the room." And the young couple told Judy that she was helping them prepare to talk to their own children about sex someday.

As Judy told us this story, she said that her beloved son and his girlfriend do not have a community in which they can talk about serious matters. And the few friends they have are simply reflecting the mythic ethos of a culture far from the social, medical, psychological and spiritual truths surrounding real sex. As she spoke, I wondered whether her son would find a church that openly and appropriately reveals itself regarding sexuality. Are there many churches like that? When in the church's place of greatest learning and greatest modeling of values (our worship services) have we celebrated the beauty and order of God's handiwork as revealed in human sexuality? Is it not the case that most worshiping communities have been silent on one of life's most important topics, while other cultural voices and images speak loudly and clearly? As one of my favorite high school teachers used to say, "Silence is construed to be consent."

Judy's story continued. After she left the young couple's house, she stopped by a local coffee shop to grab something for the long ride home. There in a corner was her son and his girlfriend. She went over and asked them if they were okay. They nodded. She said, "I don't know if the president will do anything about that housing situation, so you'd better fill out that form."

"I'm going to, Mom," he said. "I've decided I'm going to live in the dorm."

"We've decided we're going to do a lot of things differently," said his girlfriend.

Judy told us she drove home singing...

Blessed be your name
On the road marked with suffering
Though there's pain in the offering
Blessed be your name

. . . worshiping the God who cares deeply about the sex life of her son.

Marriage: Danyale's Wedding

When you can state the theme of a story, when you can separate it from the story itself, then you can be sure the story is not a very good one. The meaning of a story has to be embodied in it, has to be made concrete in it. A story is a way to say something that can't be said any other way, and it takes every word in the story to say what the meaning is.

— Flannery O'Connor
Mystery and Manners

I went to Danyale's wedding in December. If you know my friend and former student Danyale, then you probably like her. If you have just met her, then you already know her pretty well. That is because Danyale wears her personality inside out.

If she is feeling anything at all, you are going to find out about it. For example, a couple of years ago, she announced to my wife Karen and me that she had decided to go to graduate school.

"I'm going to study acting," she said. Those were the words: "I'm going to study acting." She said them quietly with a smile on her face. But along with the words was all the horror of a decision ill-made and all the hope of doing for the rest of her life what she loves so much and does so well.

"I'm going to study acting." And we all started crying. Danyale has that effect on people.

When she walks into a room, she brings her whole self. This fact makes her a great actor and sometimes gets her into trouble, since being totally committed to the present moment, she is probably going to be late for whatever moment comes next.

While she was a student at our college, the phone rang at our house after midnight one night. It was Danyale. She had been working in the quiet solitude of my office at school and had gotten caught up in her writing, and she had forgotten that they lock up the building at midnight, and could Karen or I get dressed and come and unlock the door so she did not have to spend the night there? Again.

It was this latter feature of Danyale's personality that made us wonder what we would find when we went to her wedding. I wondered, only half-facetiously, if she would actually make it to the church on time. And Karen and I both wondered about this young man that we had never met who would marry our surrogate daughter. Ironically, Danyale's mom is also named Karen. Danyale's parents divorced early, and Danyale spent much of her childhood with grandparents. By the time she graduated from college, she had acquired a stepdad she barely knew, making "home" a complex word. She lived with us for a year and a half and so transitioned from student to friend to member of the family.

But now enters Jesse. Who in the world was Jesse?

Jesse was the young man Danyale had met on a trip to Washington State. Jesse. A person who shared her passionate faith, but a person confused by her love of the theatre. And so he wrote us a letter and asked, "What place does a Christian have in the theatre?" More specifically, "How can Danyale be in that Tennessee Williams play at graduate school? How does that glorify God?"

Danyale also wrote us letters and called on the phone. She affirmed that Jesse's questions were real. They were not self-righteous attacks. It was just that he had discovered pieces of his beloved's personality that were, from his perspective, worn outside in. He wanted to know them, but they were hidden. She did not have the words. What could she say? "What is theatre supposed to do?" she wrote. "Is it different for us who call ourselves children of God? What theatre does God look upon with delight?"

Danyale had studied with us for four years. She had lived with us. We had talked for hours on end about these very things. She had chosen art over craft, drama over skit, irony over blatancy, and poetry over rhetoric. She had embraced what the writer and Christian Flannery O'Connor calls art that "reveals as much of the mystery of existence as possible." But Danyale was struggling to summarize the journey for Jesse who had not had the benefit of the experience.

I thought of Arthur Holmes, philosopher and Christian. In *The Idea of a Christian College*, he reminded us, "All truth is God's." And later on down the page, "All beauty is from God, no matter where it is found."

I also thought about my college professor Harriet Whiteman. One day I asked Professor Whiteman if she would tell me the titles of some religious plays I should read. She shot back, "All great plays are religious." I pretended, at the time, that I knew what she meant, but I did not. I now know that one of the things she was saying to me was, "You want to take the short cut, sonny, but you can't. You're gonna have to read them all." I had no shortcut for Danyale to give Jesse either. And I wondered if this young couple was moving dangerously close to the

edge of an old, old battleground—the off again, on again war
between the arts and the church.

Karen and I prayed for Danyale and Jesse. Praying for
them did not make the suspicions go away. What if Jesse turned
out to be like the girlfriend I had in college? When she discovered I was playing a character in a play who carried a cigarette,
she was appalled. She said, "What if Jesus came back today,
would you want him to catch you with that cigarette in your
hand?!!" Her theological basis for telling me to stop playing
characters who do "bad" things was from the verse in Philippians 4 that says whatever is honest, just, pure—think on these
things. If she were writing a paraphrase of the Bible, her version
of that verse would read, "Think only nice thoughts." Her Bible
would not include the rape of Tamar or Herod's slaughter of the
children.

Was Jesse like my girlfriend? Would he insist that Danyale
choose between her art and her faith? Who was Jesse?

In the spring, Danyale wrote to say, "The struggle Jesse and
I have over theatre is not over, but," she said, "it is a hopeful
struggle and maybe even a necessary one for both of us." Then
in the fall, the wedding announcement came.

We still had not met Jesse. Now we would meet him for
the first time at the wedding.

Danyale asked Karen to sing at the wedding. I was thrilled.
I was thrilled because she had not asked me. I think Danyale
has heard me say that I hate to sing in weddings because they
make me too nervous. I am always afraid I am going to make a
mistake and fifty years from now, this old couple is going to be
looking through their wedding album saying, "There's that guy
who messed up his song and ruined our wedding."

The wedding was set to take place up in the mountains
north of Seattle, close to the Canadian border. As we drove up

from the Seattle airport, I continued to think about Jesse and what he thought about Danyale and the theatre. I was listening to the radio, and a commercial came on. "Come to Christian Supply for the goodness in your life! Come in for books and gifts and prints from your favorite artists. Hot new music. Learn why thousands of northwest shoppers come into Christian Supply!" I remembered my recent trip to the Christian bookstore back home. It had a framed, matted painting for sale—a lighthouse with a beam of light cutting across the waves with words painted in the beam, "He is the light that shines in the darkness." And then in teeny-tiny print, "John 1:5a." As I stood there looking at the wall of prints and paintings, I started shaking my hands to try and relax myself. Then I noticed the clerk was looking at me really funny, so I left. But on my way out, I noticed none of the art was there as art itself. It was always in support of an idea, usually an idea plastered on its surface in the form of a Bible verse. It was like being handed a beautifully layered lasagna with a sign superglued directly on top of the cheese reading, "Lasagna is tasty and filling!" You get the idea of the lasagna but it kind of ruins the experience. I wondered if that was the kind of art to which Jesse was hoping Danyale would aspire. Who was Jesse?

On Friday evening, we arrived at the church for the rehearsal. The rehearsal was set to begin at 6:00 P.M. We arrived on time. The little country church was practically empty. Jesse's mom, Linda, was there putting up garlands of evergreen. The tiny wedding choir was practicing the old hymn of Emmanuel's land:

> *Dark, dark hath been the midnight,*
> *But dayspring is at hand.*

No Danyale. No Jesse. We worked for a while, helping Linda put up evergreens. Suddenly this guy who looked like— well, he looked like a high school kid—walked in the back door. He walked up to me. I said, "Are you Jesse?" He said, "Yeah." I shook his hand. I said, "I'm Jeff." And I could not think of another thing to say. So, I did not say anything. And neither did he.

We stood there, silent. I was trying to figure out if he was as tall as Danyale. Finally, I said, "Well, gotta get the garlands up."

Danyale finally arrived and all was well. There were many people to meet but little time for substantive interactions. "How old is Jesse?" I whispered to somebody. "You can't go by appearances," they said. "Everyone in his family looks young."

The next day was filled with busyness. In the early afternoon, Jesse's mom called to say, "Please come over to the church building to help finish decorating. I just realized that the wedding starts at 5:00 not 7:00!" We hurried over to the church to help. Before we knew it, it was 4:00. Karen dropped me at the reception hall to help finish decorating. She went back to change clothes, pick up our kids, and get my clothes for the wedding. When everyone left the reception hall at five minutes until 5:00, they asked me if I wanted a ride back to the church building. I assured them Karen was coming back for me and that I should wait. I did wait. Five o'clock came and went. No Karen.

At 5:20, I started to walk. I was not properly dressed for the bitter cold. I literally began to be afraid. But I was caught between the hope of Danyale's wedding ahead of me and the warmth of the reception hall behind. Suddenly I saw familiar headlights on the road. Karen. She had been sitting at the church building waiting for the wedding to begin, wondering what was keeping me. It had taken her a while to realize that everyone was there from the reception hall. Except me. I frantically changed clothes in the van while Karen drove us back. The thought occurred to me that we should establish precisely whose fault it was that we were the ones who were late.

An inner voice said, "Jeff, be quiet. Is it not enough that you are riding safely with the love of your life to Danyale's wedding?" I said, "Yeah, that's enough."

When we got there, the church was silent, waiting. The evergreen garlands looked glorious in the candlelight. Karen and I crept down to the front. As we sat there catching our breaths, I could not help thinking, "There's going to be this old couple fifty years from now, looking through their wedding album. And they'll come upon my picture, and they'll say, 'There's that guy who was late and ruined our wedding.'"

The wedding began, and Jesse and Danyale had prepared a thing of beauty. The tiny wedding choir sang their hymn so well.

> *The bride eyes not her garment,*
> *But her dear bridegroom's face.*
> *I will not gaze at glory,*
> *But on my King of grace.*

There was an elderly man with a gray beard seated directly behind us. He seemed odd and out of place. He wore blue jeans and a tan winter coat. Every two minutes he turned to the woman next to him and muttered, "Do I stand now?" Danyale's mother and stepdad were in the front row. Danyale had chosen to walk the aisle alone. "Do I stand now?" said the man. Karen's solo went fine until she glimpsed Danyale's handkerchief moving to her face; then those two hearts embraced from across the room, and the quality of the musical tone was no longer the important thing. "Do I stand now?" said the man, and the woman said, "Yes, now." The man stood with a Bible in his hand. His voice became miraculously strong and secure, passionate, and bold.

"This is the Word of God," he said, "our Creator, our Redeemer. Paul's letter to the Philippians." Somehow, he said it as if Paul were his own brother.

> *If there is any encouragement in Christ, any incentive of love, any participation in the Spirit, any affection or sympathy, complete my joy by being of the same mind, having the same love . . .*
>
> (Philippians 2:1–2a, RSV)

He read for some time. When the man in the tan winter coat sat down, I suspected that I had just heard the best reading of scripture ever in my life. I had not met this old man, but I felt as if I knew him; he seemed to be wearing his faith inside out.

The pastor stood up and said, "Well, Jesse. Danyale. Now you've done it. You've gone and got yourself a Christmas wedding. As if your friends didn't have enough to do this time of year." He gave a very fine wedding sermon. I especially appreciated the line, "Christian discipleship is seldom tested more completely than in marriage." That line carried a special poignancy when Jesse's dad, an ordained preacher, stood up to administer the wedding vows. Most people in the room were aware that Jesse's mom, who sat in the front pew, and Jesse's dad, who stood on the platform, had not so long ago been divorced. In this tiny church building, they were less than five feet away from Danyale's mom and stepdad. Jesse's father looked at these two young people and said, "You two know brokenness." We knew what he meant. There would be no hypocrisy here, no sweeping under the rug—thinking only nice thoughts. Only a gentle stepping forward, broken promises and brand new promises existing side by side in the presence of a mysterious grace. The old man behind me leaned forward in silence.

Late that night, Karen and I went back over the day together. We relived our open-mouthed wonder when at the wedding reception, Jesse and his brother were lovingly remembering their days as gymnasts. At the insistence of the crowd, Jesse strode to the middle of the floor and, with his brother's protective hand resting lightly on his belt, popped off a freestanding backflip, wedding tuxedo and all. And Danyale's roommate, Casey, was there. She had flown in from Ohio, where Jesse and Danyale would return so that Danyale could finish graduate school. Casey stood up and told us about a day that Jesse called for Danyale. It had been a blue day for Casey, so Jesse sang her a song over the phone, just to cheer her up.

Karen said it was Casey's story that finally convinced her that it was going to be okay. For me, it was the image of Jesse twirling around backwards in his wedding suit. Somehow, this young man had done a backflip into my heart. It was a reminder to me that there is a dramatic difference between the idea of something and the thing itself.

Death: The Other Driver

*As we sing, we learn the songs that we will hum to ourselves
in moments of deep despair. One wise pastoral musician said
that every week she leads congregational singing, she is rehearsing the congregation for a future funeral.*

— John Witvliet
Worship Seeking Understanding

"This is your mother. I really need you to call me as soon as
you get this message."

The cell phone signal was not good at the lake. But it was
good enough to tell me that my vacation was about to be over.
I made the call. It was worse than I expected. My sister and her
husband had died together. My mom knew few details: another
car coming out of nowhere, and a tumbling, bouncing violence
that no amount of seatbelts and airbags could assuage.

Because of a convolution of family scheduling needs, I
drove through six states to get to the funeral. Late in the
evening, my wife and I checked into a little Wisconsin lodge.
She went to bed in preparation for the day ahead. I stayed up,
finishing my assigned eulogy.

The next morning, we arrived early at the country church
building. The parking lot was already full, and cars were lining
the road. My sister was part of that small town demographic
where the circle of acquaintance spreads wide.

Stepping into the building, I was struck with a sight that one seldom sees—two caskets end to end. I immediately wished that we had been able to arrive in time for the visitation the night before. Now I had to process a lot of emotion in the brief span before I got up to speak.

I am a college professor of speech and theatre. I have been teaching for many years, but I had never before been called upon to write a eulogy. I wrote quickly, in a state of shock, which rather than thrusting me into an emotional turmoil, took my emotion away, transplanting it with numbness and uncertainty. But many prayed, and I applied my best years of experiences at other kinds of writing. I wanted to honor my sister and brother-in-law, but mostly I wanted to please our Lord at a moment when many hearts and minds would be vulnerable to both blessings and dangers.

Under normal circumstances, I would have wanted to work without notes. On this occasion, I did not know what sort of pressures would arise. So I talked myself into taking my entire manuscript to the podium. It did not matter. Halfway through, I could no longer see the paper. Here is my memory of what I said:

> Rissa asked if I'd say something today. I'm Rissa's Uncle Jeff. I'm Gary's brother-in-law. I'm Debbie's brother.
>
> About one year ago, I received this email:
> *Happy Birthday, Jeff. Last year in the 40s. Enjoy. Next year we'll both be old people. Not really, you're only as old as you feel. Deb.*
>
> Just a few days ago, I received this email:
> *Dear Jeff. Just wanted to wish you a happy birthday. I hear you'll be in California. . . . Hope you have a great time. And happy #50. Love. Deb.*

Little did I know that before I could visit my parents in California, I would see them here.

Debbie was one year older than me. In some places on this planet, 51 is a long life. Not here. It's not long enough. Neither is 57. It's too soon. That's how I feel today; that's how we all feel. They were too young. It was too soon.

If Debbie were here today, she'd say, "Oh, Jeff. You don't have to be so serious." And Gary would flash his great big grin and say, "No, Debba. That's what Jeff is, he's serious. You can't change that." And Debbie would say, "I know, Gary, but the Lord has been so good to us all these years—how can we ever complain?"

And there it is. That's why we all feel the way we feel. Because we want to hear those sweet voices and see those wide smiles and sit again in the presence of two people who believed with their whole hearts that every breath was a gift not to be despised and always to be cherished. Who has taught us this lesson better than these two? "Every breath is a gift not to be despised and always to be cherished."

It almost seems weird that we would learn such optimism and hope from these two. They knew life's most bitter lessons. They each had known the dark days of divorce, and the swamping waters that often swallow entire families in the wake of such brokenness. Together Gary and Debbie had faced years of job insecurity, and shortly after they started their own business, they learned that a tornado can easily engulf a town of a thousand. Then, in her fiftieth year of life, Deb was forced to look cancer in the face. "But Jeff," Debbie would say, "The Lord has been so good to us all these years—how can we ever complain?"

Gary and Debbie loved the Bible, and I have an impulse to claim that they, through their trials, were living examples of these words from James: "Consider it pure joy my brother and sister whenever you face trials of many kinds, because you know that the testing of your faith develops perseverance." Gary and Debbie certainly had perseverance. And they certainly had joy. But I'm not sure it was because of their trials. I don't know what Gary was like as a boy, but I grew up with Debbie. And my recollection is that she always had joy and perseverance. She will be remembered by her seven brothers and sisters as the sweetest person we ever knew. She was a woman without guile. And it's not clear to me that she needed trials to develop that. She was rather a miraculous gift to the rest of us, calling us to come through our own trials, because we could see her there on the other side.

When Debbie was in the fourth grade, she was what we called back then, "put back." At the time, I'm sure it seemed like the end of the world. But for me it meant that when I started fourth grade, there she was with me. And she stayed beside me all the way through high school. Every year, after fourth grade, when all the children started a new year with the normal feelings of anxiety, I had my sister Debbie starting school with me, and I faced the trial of each new year with a sense of "at homeness" and I was stronger for it. I had my sister. I wasn't alone. And on graduation day, they called my sister's name and then mine. She was with me to the end.

Next year, I will become the age my sister is now. She has been put back, and I will catch up with her.

And as I move through life, I will have her with me, as she is now. I will remember her as she was the last time I saw her—radiant, joyous, the sweetest person I ever knew.

You can see them, can't you? You each have your own images. And you can hear the echoes of their gentle laughs—Debbie's like a morning bird, Gary's like a country road. You know that they are telling us to keep loving each other, and keep forgiving each other. It is right that these two great souls finally found each other and had more than two decades together. They were indeed, each of them, miraculous gifts calling to the rest of us to come through our own trials and meet them on the other side.

As we filed solemnly out of the church building, my twenty-something nephew from Illinois broke from the line and came to embrace me. "Thank you for what you said about my mom. Someone needed to say the way she was." He returned to the line. I thought of him through the rest of the day. His own journey following the divorce had been a long hard road. And I thought of another long hard road—the future path of the young man, a boy really, who was driving the other car. He was not at the funeral. His journey was separate from ours. But his grief was surely just as great, if not greater. What about him?

We buried them. My brother-in-law was a veteran, so I witnessed the speech that veterans say on behalf of the President of the United States to the grieving mother as they present the folded flag.

We returned for the luncheon, and then I got back on the road. I had a long evening's drive which would put me on the California flight that my sister had referenced in her final email.

Six days later, on Father's Day, the seven remaining siblings gathered at my parents' Santa Ana home. Of this group, only my parents and I had been able to attend the funeral. Now we needed another memorial service of some kind. I read them the eulogy I had given as their representative. My father prayed a Father's Day prayer that no father wishes to pray. But it was true, we said.

The next day, we hung out in smaller groups. We watched a movie. We said, "Try this guacamole, it's good." Late in the evening we verbally sorted through some of the details of the traffic accident that had taken those two lives. I was the only sibling that had been there at the site, so I told them what I had seen. I told about going to see the vehicle in storage. I wondered aloud about the nineteen year old who was driving the other car. My sister Chris said, "I've wondered about him, too." "Do we know his name?" I asked. "It's on the internet," said Jane. "I don't like that our legal system keeps us separate from him," I said. "He's a part of this with us. He has healing to do, and we are a part of that process for him." Jane said, "Honestly, I haven't thought about him yet." Understandable.

Chris came over to see me the morning before I left California. She had something to say, so we took a walk up the street. "My daughter once ran her car into another car," she said. "She caused very little damage to the other car, but the people have been very mean about it. It's years now, but they're still trying to sue our insurance company for the emotional trauma that my daughter's hit on their bumper has caused their marriage. They say they can't be intimate anymore, and it all started with that hit on their bumper. They say that's worth at least $40,000." My sister paused. Then she said, "That young man driving the truck that hit Debbie, that young man has a mother. I don't want to fight them. I don't want anyone to try and put a price on my sister's life."

When we got back to my parents, the phone rang. It was one of my brothers. He asked me if I was going to be around, because he wanted to talk. I said our parents and I were going to be gone for the day. (I could not bear to tell him that we were going to Disneyland—that seemed so ridiculous under the circumstances. But at the moment, I needed ridiculous.) My brother said all he wanted to say was that he wondered if I had thought at all about the young man driving that truck. "He needs to hear from us," my brother said. "He probably feels pretty messed up about this, and we shouldn't hate him." I said, "Remember the line in the eulogy I wrote—where I said I thought Gary and Debbie would want us to keep loving each other and keep forgiving each other?" "Yes!" he said. I confessed that I did not feel it was my place to tell others how to feel about that young man, but I wanted to make a gesture of some kind. Something. My brother said, "Maybe you should poll the family." I said I did not think I would do that. He said, "Well, if you want to write to him, you can speak for me, too."

All that was last week. This week, my sister Chris has gone home to Maui. My brother Jon is back in Seattle. My dad is back to work in California. My mom is in New York for a flower show. I am back home in Iowa. I have not written to the young man yet. I do not know why. But I have said prayers for him. And I have thought of him. And I have told myself that I will write soon.

The phone rings. It is my mom, with this story. It is hard to believe.

On her way to New York, my mom stopped by Wisconsin to touch base with my deceased sister's nineteen-year-old daughter, Rissa. Rissa is now home alone. But today, my mom is there. They get up on this Monday morning and they say, what should we do today? "I don't know," says Rissa. My mom explains that some of the California family want pictures of the crash site. "Let's drive over to Hayward for lunch," says my mom, "And we'll stop and take some pictures." They invite my sister's best friend, Scheryl, to go along.

At the site, they get their pictures. The scars in the earth, where the vehicle bounced and rolled. The two little plastic crosses where the vehicle came to rest. Rissa does not know who put them there last week, but her mom and dad were much beloved in their little town, so it could have been any number of people. Now, though, something is different. "Look," says Rissa. "There are flowers planted next to the crosses." And the three women notice that someone has carefully mowed the grass in this long section of the ditch.

They go to Hayward. They have lunch. Before they start out on the hour-long ride back to Siren, they stop to buy some bottles of water. It takes a while to get the water at a convenience store. Scheryl is a little frustrated with the wait. She wants to get going.

At last, they get going, and, of course, they pass the site once again. A vehicle is stopped by the road, and someone is standing in the ditch. Who is that, the women wonder. "I'm going to find out," says Scheryl, and she turns the car around.

Now I am about to tell you something you should not use in court. I am not creating a legal document. I was not there. I am simply telling you a story, consolidating a couple of ways that it was reported to me, trying to recreate the story as best I can, trying to keep a memory that's not my own, trying to make it mine, trying to give it to you.

They get back to the site, and they see that it is a young man and a young woman. By now, the young man is back in the passenger seat of the car, sitting alone. They pull up close enough to him for Scheryl to call out, "Did you know them?"

He shakes his head and asks, "Did you?" Rissa speaks, "They were my parents." He gets out of the car.

He walks over to Rissa's window. His first words are, "I am so sorry." They are words he repeats a dozen times during the very brief conversation. "I never saw them," he says. "I wish I could take it back. I get up every morning and wish it could be gone. I stopped at the stop sign. I started across the highway. I was going to work for my dad, landscaping. And then I was hit, and I was spun around. And when I stopped, I looked and I saw them. Their car tumbling. And I got out and ran over to them. They were upside down and they weren't moving at all. Someone had called 911. They got here very fast. It was only about three minutes. It seemed like forever. They ran over to me and I said, don't worry about me—go over there. And they went and looked and then they started getting them out. And then they went back and got the body bags, and I said, no, no, no, this can't be."

My mom tells me that Rissa is very calm. Rissa says to the young man, "I had been wanting to talk to you."

The young man says, "I'm afraid to go into town. I'm afraid to talk to anyone. People think I'm a killer." He looks over at the young woman with him. "My sister drives me everywhere. I haven't driven yet." He gestures to the ditch. "I will continue to take care of this crash site. I'll keep it looking nice. I'll keep it mowed. There are wood ticks out here—I want you to be able to come out here whenever you want and not have to worry." Then he remembers something. "When I was mowing, I saw something shiny in the grass. It was a bracelet. I don't know if it was something that you . . . I hung it on one of the crosses."

My mom gets out and goes over to the cross, leaving Rissa talking to Josh, who explains that he has an appointment and needs to leave. And now there are cars slowing down along the highway. My mom finds the bracelet and brings it back and hands it to Rissa. "That's my mom's bracelet," she says. Scheryl gasps and says, "I've got the other one at home. Debbie and I bought a matching set." Rissa puts it on.

My mom tells me over the phone that Josh had said he is tired of people telling him it was meant to be. Why should he have to be part of such a plan, he wonders. I tell her I understand Josh's question. I find strange solace in what Isaiah said, that even our right acts are old rags in the face of God's glory. God's reclaiming work in creation is ongoing, the same work on tragic days as well as good days. Beyond that I profess no special knowledge of what was meant at that particular Wisconsin intersection. Nevertheless, I am glad for the quirky detail of a sluggish convenience store stop that, at last, brought two nineteen-year-olds and two families face to face.

It is now a year later. The official police report has arrived at my home. It includes an on-site interview with the other driver, designated in the report as "Unit Number 1." There in a shaky hand are his answers to the printed questions.

> How fast were you traveling?
> *10 mph.*
>
> What indicated to you that an accident would occur?
> *No.*
>
> Did you do anything to avoid this accident, i.e., braking, turning, etc.?
> *Never saw them.*
>
> In your opinion, why did this accident occur?
> *I don't know.*

Heaven: The Fourposter

Human honors are a natural by-product of heaven's honors.
— Professor Kenneth Brashier
2006 National Professor of the Year, Reed College

Karen and I met at Greenville College. The theatre professor there was Margo Voltz. Margo cast Karen and me as Amanda and Tom in *The Glass Menagerie*, and the embers of our friendship grew bright as we whispered backstage during the long Jim and Laura scene in Act II.

Margo was married to David Mellick, a philosophy professor at Greenville. Margo and David opened their home to us. Rehearsal would move naturally from the theatre to their living room for tea and conversation. While Karen and I were falling for each other, we were learning about the intertwining of love and faith, art and worship, and learning and living by watching David and Margo up close.

By the end of my junior year, Margo had mentored me into a desire to study theatre seriously, but there was no theatre major at Greenville. In addition, the temporary assignments David and Margo had at Greenville were coming to an end. They would be looking for work elsewhere. It was a time for transition. (Little did I know it was one of the last times we would see David on this earth. At age thirty-nine, he would die of cancer. Suddenly. But that is mostly a separate story.)

Karen and I got married and moved to Seattle where I could get a theatre major at Greenville's sister school, Seattle Pacific University. For our first apartment, our brother-in-law had given us an old table top with no legs. We put it on a large cardboard box and it became our kitchen table. I built kitchen chairs out of two-by-fours, modeled after chairs I had seen at the Pier One Imports store down near the Pike Place Market. I actually went down there with my tape measure to filch their design. I built a sofa out of two-by-sixes. Karen made some cushions. For our bed we had an old mattress, but no bed frame, so we slept on the floor. We were poor, but happy.

Another year passed, and we found ourselves returning to Greenville for Karen to teach at the high school where she had earlier done her student teaching. We brought along our motley collection of furniture, but now that we were both working, we were ready to make some changes.

During this time, we started a little theatre company and produced the two-person play *The Fourposter*. We received permission to use the college's theatre which was dark during Greenville's January interterm. We needed a fourposter bed to do the play, and we still needed a bed for our own apartment. We decided to solve both of these problems by purchasing a bed. We would first use it in the play and then take it home after striking the play. But we did not have enough money to purchase an antique fourposter bed that would fit the period of the play, and we agreed that, for this project, we could not depend on my skills with a circular saw and knotty pine. Then we heard that the college's chemistry professor did a little woodworking on the side. We went to him and explained our situation. As I recall, he was teaching a special interterm class on woodworking. He said if we would pay for the lumber, he would give the bed to his students as a project, saving us a great deal of money. We agreed, as long as he would have the bed delivered by first dress rehearsal. We were set.

We went into rehearsal, and the professor, whose name was Frank Wiseman, went to a local sawmill and picked up rough-hewn walnut which he and his students took home and planed. They glued the boards together and cut them and lathed them. This process took a long time. The students were done with their class before the bed was done. The professor said he would finish it himself for no extra charge. All of us had clearly bitten off more than we could chew. I was in over my head doing everything that it takes to start a theatre company, learn my lines, and sell a few tickets. I could not afford to help Frank or let him off the hook. We would all just have to do our best.

I do not know how many nights Frank was up late building that bed, but he did deliver it on time. It did not have any varnish yet, but each night after dress rehearsals, he came and applied more varnish, and it was finally shiny and dry on opening night. It turned out to be a lovely production, and on closing night, we took the bed home.

At the end of that year, we moved away to start graduate school. We took all that cobbled up furniture and one beautiful bed. We crafted a life combining teaching, theatre and worship leading. We disposed of all our start-up furniture except that bed.

We have that bed to this day.

Now the story jumps ahead three decades. In 2006, I received a letter telling me I had been selected Iowa Professor of the Year. The award came with an invitation to Washington, DC, for a special luncheon with all the other state winners and also the four national winners.

Professor of the Year. What do you do with that? One does not expect such things. Might as well try to win the lottery. And then you win it. You roll your eyes, knowing there are so many teachers more deserving. But it is an opportunity to attract attention to one's college and colleagues. Our college's public relations department struggles long and hard to point out that this institution is not only viable, but remarkable. Awards provide a palpable symbol of that reality.

But what of God? How does this bring God glory? What do human honors have to do with honoring heaven? How does worship of God continue when the applause is directed toward you?

I have seen some Christians answer the above questions by waving down the applause. I have heard of singers who chastised audiences at their concerts when they applauded. And I have had performers say to me, "Don't thank me! Give the praise to the Lord!" I have wondered what it is like to live in relationship with such folks. Pass the peas, please. Here you go. Thank you. Oh, don't thank me, praise the Lord who made these peas for us to enjoy!

Didactic responses can be relationship-stoppers. I prefer a simpler response to the world's honors: you just say thank you. There are many reasons to be grateful when someone reaches out to you with care and graciousness. These gracious words are the currency of relationship. And once we have relationship, then there is opportunity to explore where we have come from and where we are going. Values and beliefs can be shared and affirmed. Then the truth can come into focus. I am speaking now of the truth that it is not really us who sits in the seat of honor. We sit there on behalf of the Lord who gave us life and ability, and also on behalf of those leaders and teachers who gave of themselves so we could flourish. When we can reflect the light of this truth back upon those others, then joy will follow.

Let me show you what I mean.

Remember David and Margo? As I was being interviewed prior to my trip to Washington for this award, I mentioned David and Margo. They were a shining example of the interplay of learning and living that guides my model of education, and I wanted to acknowledge them as one of the primary sources of my own understanding of what it means to be a college professor. On the day of the announcement of the professors of the year in the nation's capitol, media around the country released their stories. My own story showed up in a few Iowa venues, most especially the newspapers in what we who live in this area call "Siouxland." It was across the Missouri River in the Sioux Falls *Argos Leader* that Jill Callison, the religion editor, included my mention of David and Margo.

I know my story is a bit rambling, but hang with me. It will pay off.

On the morning of the luncheon in Washington, the *Argos Leader* posted their story to the web. When I saw that the article mentioned Margo and David, I quickly sent the following email to New Mexico:

Margo,

If you'll click on this link and scroll down to the bottom article (Sioux Falls *Argos Leader*), you'll see your name in the article, and I'm so proud that it's there.

http://www.nwciowa.edu/news/contentID.1718/article.aspx

With gratitude for you and David in my life,

Jeff

I was too late. Through the magic of search engines, a person can have the web automatically find any new mention of their family name and send them an email about it. David's brother received one of these emails, and contacted Margo before I did. Here is part of her email response to me:

> Jeff!
>
> I am overwhelmed. But someone "scooped" you. One of David's brothers, Gary, called me this morning at about 6:45 to tell me that I should get on the computer to check out what "some student" had to say about David and me. After Don and I had checked it all out, I went back to the inbox and discovered your message.
>
> You and Karen have been busy since I saw you last—to say the least. I am so proud of you both! Sometimes I feel a little blue about the turns my life has taken and wish that I could have taught longer than the 2 wonderful years David and I spent at Greenville.
>
> I had planned to get my flu shot today but I don't want to spoil this kiss of Heaven. . . .
>
> Give my love to Karen and save some for yourself.
>
> Margo

Do you see what I mean? We can reflect the light back. But there is more. Later that day, I received this email from another of David's brothers:

> Dear Jeff,
>
> My brother, Dr. Gary Mellick, sent me a Google Alert relating to the newspaper article concerning your

award and the mention of brother David's name. It means so much to us to hear from others the impact David (and Margo) had in their lives. I miss David every day and as a brother, he was my primary mentor. When I make art or music, it's as though I'm working for two.

Congratulations on your award and thank you for sharing it with my brother and sister-in-law. In this way, you have shared the honor with us.

Jim Mellick

Why would you not want to win all sorts of awards if you could use them to honor those who gave so much to you? One of the reasons God teaches us to worship him is to turn us outward and thus become conduits of gratitude in every aspect of our lives. This patterning of gratefulness is gospel work, for the watching world says, "Look—how they love one another!"

Back to Washington. We met so many lovely people. Efran greeted us from behind the front desk at the Melrose Hotel on the western end of the same street that goes past the White House. Vivian was the hostess that night at The Landmark restaurant where Rose served us so graciously. It had been a long couple of days getting ready for the trip, so Karen slept in the first morning. I walked across the street and bought her a chai latte from Sam, the Asian man who runs the little coffee shop there. After getting ready for our big day, we sat on the sofa and prayed together as we do almost every day. Karen prayed that we would be a blessing to each and every person we met that day—hoping toward that wild ideal that they might look at us and catch a glimpse of Someone else.

On the way to the Willard Intercontinental on the eastward end of Pennsylvania Avenue, we chatted with the driver, Ahmed, an electrical engineer from the Sudan, currently between free-lance jobs in his main field. Since I had written a play about the Sudan, I enjoyed asking about Nasir and the Sobat River.

At the Willard, we were allowed to choose our own seats at the luncheon. We spotted a table with two young boys and went straight for them. They turned out to be Trenton and Parker, sons of Jennifer and John, and grandsons to Trina who was also with them. Jennifer was the state winner from Texas. Parker drew a Star Wars picture in my journal during the speeches. When Parker said goodbye to Karen he said, "I hope I get to see you again."

After the festivities, they asked all the state winners to gather at the front for a picture. I ended up in the center of the middle row, and the photographer asked us to angle toward the middle so we could all fit. This put me nearly nose to nose with the senior professor who was the winner from Kentucky. Then a fuse blew, and the photographer said to wait just a minute. It seemed an appropriate time for conversation. It went as follows.

IOWA
Where do you teach?

KENTUCKY
Georgetown College.

IOWA
How long have you been there?

KENTUCKY
Twenty-six years.

IOWA
And where before that?

KENTUCKY
Oh . . . a little school in Illinois. Not too far from St.
Louis.

IOWA
(getting a glimmer of suspicion)
What college?

KENTUCKY
Greenville.

IOWA
Greenville College! I was a student there.

KENTUCKY
(raised eyebrows)
Oh. When?

IOWA
I was there in the early seventies. What's your name?

KENTUCKY
Frank.

IOWA
(still not getting it)
What did you teach?

KENTUCKY
Chemistry.

IOWA

Oh. Well, that explains why I don't remember you. I was into theatre.

KENTUCKY

Oh. I didn't often go to the plays. But I built a bed for a play once.

IOWA

(Suddenly it's clear.)
That's our bed! You're Frank Wiseman. You built the bed that's still in our bedroom today.

And suddenly the photographer was back. And we were smiling for that picture.

Frank and I rushed together to the back of the room to share this story with our wives. That night, at the congressional reception, Frank found me again and said he had told his brother-in-law our story. His brother-in-law, who loves mathematics, said, "Frank, figure the odds."

Jesus said he would prepare us a place, and when he has it ready, he will welcome us to it. My sense is that one of our great activities in that heavenly place will be telling stories, connecting the dots. And God will delight, receiving our storytelling in honor of what he has been up to forever.

APPENDICES

Advent Service:
A Walk with the Shepherds

Here is an example of a worship service that includes a contemporary retelling of a Bible story interwoven with congregational singing. The songs chosen are a mixture of classic carols and older choruses. This worship script was prepared originally for the second Sunday of Advent, and we used this service on that particular Sunday for several years. One year, we used the shepherd story and song section for our Christmas Eve service.

Trinity Reformed Church at worship,
Sunday morning, December 4, 2005
Loving God by Remembering His Story

7:00 A.M. — sound check with musicians
7:15 A.M. — run through
8:00 — prayer (gather by table)
8:15 — the room is set for worship; CD plays

MUSIC AS WE PREPARE
8:30/ 10:45

"This Child" (v. 1, solo)

LIGHTING THE JOSEPH CANDLE

The candles represent Mary, Joseph, Elizabeth, John the Baptist, and the Christ child. Today, the candle is lit by . . .

"This Child" (v. 2, all)

PASTOR JON O.

In the fullness of time, a child secretly comes in the night. His way is foretold by angels and prepared for many generations. His relative Elizabeth shouts with the Holy Ghost, and John, his cousin, leaps for joy. A new day rises upon us all, like the sun. It is heaven—come down. It is the fullness of time. And today, the story brings us to some shepherds. The gospel of Luke starts the story like this (recite Luke 2: 8–14). Let's pray.

PRAYER, FOLLOWED BY WORDS OF WELCOME

If you're able, would you stand and bless each other with your greetings.

*BLESSING EACH OTHER WITH OUR GREETINGS

"This Child" (v. 3)

JEFF: If you've been around Trinity church awhile, you know that we often include in our celebration of Christmas an imaginary walk with the shepherds. We're going to take that walk today. We will use our imaginations along with some songs that we love to sing to help us put ourselves into the story. We'll follow the shepherds on the journey they took into the wee hours of that first Christmas morning.

– organ begins –

"Angels We Have Heard on High" (v. 1, v. 3)

– piano plays refrain again and modulates and plays introduction to next song –

You may be seated. After peeking in and out of a few barns and finding only cows and camels, we come upon a man leaning tiredly against a barn door, staring at the sky. We say, "Hello," and feeling just a little bit silly, we ask him if he's seen any babies around here. He just stares at us suspiciously and stays firmly planted in front of the barn door. One of us finally says, "We're looking for a baby asleep in a feed box." The man's eyes open wide, and he asks us, "Who you been talkin' to?"

We tell him, "A sky full of singing angels."

The man smiles knowingly, as if to say, "Well, why didn't you say so?" He says we'll find his wife Mary inside with the Baby, and we step in out of the cold. In the next minute, we get our first glimpse of the Savior.

"What Child Is This?" (3 vv.)

– modulate and play through next song –

This is it! It's finally happened. Prophecy fulfilled. This is the "El"—meaning "God"—who is "emmanu"—meaning, "who is with us." He is "Emannu-el." He is with us—God.

"Emmanu-el" (once)

One of us looks at Mary, the young mother, and asks, "Has his father told you his name yet?"

Mary replies, "An angel visited each of us and told us. His name is Jesus."

Those who have grown up around Bethlehem are very startled by this reply. First of all because a woman is helping choose the name, and secondly that the name is so—well, it's so ordinary. It is a much used, common name around these parts. We maybe expected her to say, "His father will call him Elijah, or Isaiah, or even Solomon." Not just another Jesus.

But suddenly we realize there's ordinary in abundance around here. An ordinary stable, an ordinary carpenter, an ordinary name, and even us. It wasn't Herod or Caesar Augustus who was invited to this bedside.

As we gather around him, standing, slouching, kneeling, sitting, staring, gawking, we are overwhelmed by the fact that the "Is With Us God" has filled the ordinary with himself.

"Jesus, Name Above All Names" (once)

– gentle modulation and sustain –

"Jesus, The Very Thought of Thee" (vv. 1–2 becomes *a capella*)

– piano plays tag –

Huddled together in the middle of the night in a musty stable, we look at each other in amazement that we are participating in this.

– modulate and play introduction –

"Isn't He Beautiful"

As we get up to go back outside, we realize that we now have something in common with Moses. We too have seen God. But this time, the "is with us God" with the ordinary name no longer asks us to remove our shoes.

"Holy Ground" (once, and then Jeff invites people to stand for a second time through)

– modulate and vamp –

We slip out into the ordinary night, but we can't yet get ourselves to leave. We're drawn back to the lighted window for one last look. And then we head back up the Judean hillside—half walking, half dancing—knowing that our lives are going to be changed forever, and that it's only just beginning. If you're able, would you stand!

*"Shine, Jesus, Shine" (v. 1, R, v. 3, R, R, Tag)

*PRAYER   Pastor Jon N.

OFFERING
[Offertory done by Alex and Cassie]

SCRIPTURE   Matthew 1:1–17

MESSAGE   In the Fullness of Time: Generations
                            Pastor Jon N.
THE LORD'S SUPPER
(include prayers of the people: conclude with Lord's Prayer)

[Elders should be instructed to come forward when ready—
NOT to wait until a song break]

Pastor Jon O: We have begun our celebration of Christ's first
coming. And we wait in hope of his second. Even so, come Lord
Jesus. And the grace of our Lord Jesus Christ be with you all.
Amen.

* *"Alleluia, He is Coming"* (final verse, R, R)

[This is on Power Point.]
(shouted)
Leader: Maranatha!
Congregation: Come quickly, Lord Jesus!

Music as we leave

*Indicates congregation standing

The Bands of Syria

Here is an example of the staging of an ancient drama of the Hebrew people. It is verbatim from 2 Kings 6:8–23, KJV.

VOCALIST

PERCUSSIONIST

STORYTELLER

KING OF SYRIA

KING OF ISRAEL

ISRAELITE SOLDIER

SYRIAN SOLDIER

SYRIAN ARCHER

ELISHA

ELISHA'S SERVANT

AT RISE: Two stools create the Israelite King's throne, and one stool is in Elisha's house.

Music begins the play. A solo voice, no lyrics, no recognizable melody. This voice will later be joined by percussion. After percussion has joined, actors enter to three separate locations.

At the start of the play, there are depictions of three separate tableaux. At stage left is Elisha's cottage, with his servant serving the evening meal. At center, is the King of Israel, with a soldier kneeling to serve something to the King. This image is the most important one, since it is the opposite of what we'll see the King doing near the end of the play. At stage right is the King of Syria preparing to go to war.

The Storyteller moves in among these three tableaux, noticing each one, and then begins the play.

STORYTELLER
Then the king of Syria warred against Israel.

(SYRIAN SOLDIER and SYRIAN ARCHER move into position to receive the plan. KING OF SYRIA kneels pointing to the place where the secret attack will be encamped.
NOTE regarding narration and image: In general, the movement to another position happens *prior* to the narrative description of what that position represents. Since this production uses frozen images or tableaux, the actors will usually remain in tableau except when they speaking or in required action as indicated.)

STORYTELLER (continued)
And took counsel with his servants, saying:

KING OF SYRIA
(pointing)
In such and such a place shall be my camp.

(SYRIAN SOLDIER moves into position of hiding to attack. SYRIAN ARCHER and KING OF SYRIA freeze in worship of their god. ELISHA'S SERVANT moves to bow in the presence of the KING OF ISRAEL.)

STORYTELLER
And the man of God sent unto the king of Israel, saying:

ELISHA'S SERVANT
Beware that thou pass not such a place; for thither the Syrians are come down.

(ELISHA'S SERVANT departs. KING OF ISRAEL speaks to ISRAELITE SOLDIER.)

STORYTELLER
And the king of Israel sent to the place which the man of God told him and warned him of.

(KING OF ISRAEL prays upstage. ISRAELITE SOLDIER approaches the place of attack, and the SYRIAN SOLDIER springs up, quickly running him through with a sword. This is mimed. SYRIAN SOLDIER thinks he has killed the Israelite King, but when he raises the man's visor, he is disheartened.
Note: all props are mimed, no period costumes are necessary, and any actor can play either male or female characters. In other words, the emphasis is on the story-

telling, not any sort of realism.)

STORYTELLER
And saved himself there, not once nor twice.

(SYRIAN SOLDIER returns to bow before his king.)

STORYTELLER (continued)
Therefore the heart of the king of Syria was sore troubled for
this thing; and he called his servants, and said unto them:

KING OF SYRIA
(threatening his soldier with a knife to the throat)
Will ye not shew me which of us is for the king of Israel?

(SYRIAN ARCHER rushes in to bow before the king, but
also to attempt to save his fellow soldier's life, even to the
point of grabbing the king's hand. They all remain in this
death grip through the next soldier's line.)

STORYTELLER
And one of his servants said:

SYRIAN SOLDIER
None, my lord, O king: but Elisha, the prophet that is in Israel,
telleth the king of Israel the words that thou speakest in thy bed-
chamber.

(KING OF SYRIA rises, angry, yells, and flings the knife
away. The soldiers and the STORYTELLER all flinch and
turn away for a moment.
    The storyteller may get involved in the action as a

human character. For example, when the two soldiers are trying to keep the king of Syria from committing a murder, the storyteller can represent a third soldier. In a later scene, we will see the storyteller representing the power of God.

When the KING OF SYRIA collects himself, he kneels to speak again to his soldiers.)

STORYTELLER

And he said:

KING OF SYRIA

Go and spy where he is, that I may send and fetch him.

(KING OF SYRIA prepares for war, as does his archer. The SYRIAN SOLDIER sneaks upstage. ELISHA stands watching. He knows that someone is coming looking for him. The SYRIAN SOLDIER finally sees ELISHA and ducks down and sneaks home to speak to the KING OF SYRIA. The SYRIANS all gather around a map on the floor, and the SYRIAN Soldier points to the precise place of ELISHA'S home.)

STORYTELLER

And it was told him, saying:

SYRIAN SOLDIER

Behold, he is in Dothan.

(SOLDIERS get ready to go to war; the KING OF SYRIA sends them with a gesture of great power.)

STORYTELLER
Therefore sent he thither horses, and chariots, and a great host.

(KING OF SYRIA lies down to sleep at his own home. EL-
ISHA and his servant are also asleep. SYRIAN SOLDIER
and SYRIAN ARCHER have arrived at Dothan, and freeze
in waiting. They are upstage of the sleeping ELISHA and
servant. In this next scene, use split focus—with ELISHA
and servant looking straight front to "see" the distant soldiers who are physically standing just behind them.)

STORYTELLER (continued)
And they came by night, and compassed the city about.

(ELISHA'S SERVANT gets up and goes to the window.)

STORYTELLER (continued)
And when the servant of the man of God was risen early, and
gone forth,

(ELISHA'S SERVANT, sees the Syrian army and ducks
down in terror.)

STORYTELLER (continued)
Behold, an host compassed the city both with horses and chariots.

(ELISHA'S SERVANT goes and wakes ELISHA.)

STORYTELLER (continued)
And his servant said unto him:

ELISHA'S SERVANT
Alas, my master! How shall we do?

(ELISHA crosses to the window and looks out at the army.)

STORYTELLER
And he answered:

ELISHA
Fear not: for they that be with us are more than they that be with them.

(ELISHA prays for his servant by placing his hand over his eyes.)

STORYTELLER
And Elisha prayed, and said:

ELISHA
LORD, I pray thee, open his eyes, that he may see.

(ELISHA removes his hand.)

STORYTELLER
And the LORD opened the eyes of the young man.

(ELISHA'S SERVANT opens his eyes and he sees the chariots of fire up and away behind the Syrians! He responds to this awesome sight, and so does ELISHA.)

STORYTELLER (continued)
And he saw: and, behold, the mountain was full of horses and
chariots of fire round about Elisha.

(SYRIAN SOLIDER draws his sword, and the SYRIAN
ARCHER draws back an arrow on his bow to shoot.)

STORYTELLER (continued)
And when they came down to him, Elisha prayed unto the
LORD, and said:

ELISHA
(ELISHA raises his arms to pray.)
Smite this people, I pray thee, with blindness.

(The storyteller can help create the miraculous influence
of God with a gesture. In this case, it is a dance-like gesture of the storyteller during the next line that causes the
Syrian soldiers to drop their weapons, having lost their
sight.)

STORYTELLER
And he smote them with blindness according to the word of Elisha.

(ELISHA and his servant move upstage to the soldiers.
ELISHA grabs one of their hands, and the servant gets in
between them, grabbing both hands, creating a line.)

STORYTELLER (continued)
And Elisha said unto them:

ELISHA

This is not the way, neither is this the city.

(ELISHA begins to move, pulling the line along behind
him in a large circle around his house.)

ELISHA (continued)

Follow me, and I will bring you to the man whom ye seek.

STORYTELLER

But he led them to Samaria.

(The line arrives at Samaria, where the KING OF ISRAEL
is now awake and waiting, starting to pick up a bow and
arrow.)

STORYTELLER (continued)

And it came to pass, when they were come into Samaria, that
Elisha said:

ELISHA

LORD, open the eyes of these men, that they may see.

(ELISHA and his servant move away, leaving the soldiers
on their own, blind and frightened. Again, the STORY-
TELLER gestures the miracle.)

STORYTELLER

And the LORD opened their eyes, and they saw.

(The Syrian soldiers sink in despair, knowing they have
been trapped and are going to be killed.)

STORYTELLER (continued)
And, behold, they were in the midst of Samaria.

(ELISHA moves around to stage right of the KING OF IS-
RAEL, who looks at the soldiers and prepares to draw his
bow toward them.)

STORYTELLER (continued)
And the king of Israel said unto Elisha, when he saw them:

KING OF ISRAEL
(drawing his bow)
My father, shall I smite them? Shall I smite them?

(ELISHA rushes around to the King's left so that he is
now between the King and the Syrian soldiers. The King
lowers his bow so that ELISHA is not in danger.)

STORYTELLER
And he answered:

ELISHA
Thou shalt not smite them: wouldest thou smite those whom
thou hast taken captive with thy sword and with thy bow? Set
bread and water before them, that they may eat and drink, and
go to their master.

(The KING OF ISRAEL now has a decision to make. He
attempts to get ELISHA to back down by threatening
him, pointing the bow directly at him! The percussion
builds to a furious climax and stops. There is frozen silence as we wait for one of the two powerful leaders to

back down. Finally there is a sharp click with a percussive instrument. Then one more, and the KING OF ISRAEL backs down. He sets his bow aside and moves to stage left to get some food for the soldiers. ELISHA'S SERVANT gets the idea, and leads the Syrian soldiers upstage to sit on the KING OF ISRAEL'S throne. The King brings them food, kneeling to them. ELISHA and his servant also kneel. The soldiers finally decide to reach for the food, and there is a freeze.)

STORYTELLER

And he prepared great provision for them.

(The soldiers are finished feasting, and they get up and leave, one of them turning to raise a hand to wave to the King who also raises a hand to wave.)

STORYTELLER (continued)

And when they had eaten and drunk, he sent them away.

(The Syrian soldiers kneel at the side of their own King, who partially sits up, listening to their amazing story. Freeze.)

STORYTELLER (continued)

And they went to their master.

(Now all are up and starting to move slowly offstage in opposite directions, Syrians to the right, and Israelites to the left. The two kings pause and turn their heads to look at one another. Freeze.)

STORYTELLER (continued)
So the bands of Syria came no more into the land of Israel.

(STORYTELLER moves upstage, all turn offstage and take
a step or two and freeze, and hold until final vocal tone
and final click of percussion signals the end of the play.)

Story into Drama:
A Model

The script of my play *Sioux Center Sudan* can be found on-line. It models some specific techniques that are helpful for turning stories into dramas within the context of worship. I commend the following for your consideration.

1. *A true story:* The scriptures are jammed full of true stories of God at work in the lives of his people. This pattern is one of remembrance. God remembers us, and we remember God. It is crucial that our worship reflects this pattern of remembering. One of the ways we remember is by including true stories from scripture and from contemporary life. As I have mentioned earlier, we can do so simply, but sometimes we do so by placing reality under the microscope of our best artistic techniques.

2. *Music:* Most cultures from ancient Greece to modern film have told their stories to a sound-track. Using two artistic languages at the same time can make them each more powerful.

3. Narration: This device is an ancient one. It disappeared in the 1800s when realism came into fashion. It returned in the twentieth century with playwrights Thornton Wilder, Bertolt Brecht and Paul Sills. It is valuable for stories that cover a lot of time and space. It is especially valuable for most worship settings in which there are other activities that segue into and out of the storytelling. It is also a helpful way to acknowledge the presence and participation of the congregation in worship.

4. Theatricality—acknowledging the use of the audience's imagination to create the world of the story: A variety of evocative devices are used in *Sioux Center Sudan*. Some of these are mimed props, simple stools to represent things like a jeep and an airplane, actors remaining visible onstage throughout, doubled actors, avoidance of typecasting (cutting across age, gender, and ethnicity), hints of costume. Using an imaginative theatricality is more practical than realism and, to my taste, more satisfying artistically.

5. Tableaux: The frozen image is, of course, another example of theatricality. The power of this imagery is so valuable that it deserves special mention.

6. Offstage focus: I am referring to actors looking offstage to play a scene, as if their scene partner is out in space in the center of the audience. We sometimes forget that we can "move the camera." This device helps the audience see the actors better and it serves to further engage our imaginations. Remember also that you can change the vertical focus as well as the horizontal focus.

7. *Respect for cultural heritage without leaving out the uninitiated:* If a play includes scripture, songs and events from Christian tradition, none of these should be so jargonized that non-Christians cannot appreciate the value of the story. This is achieved by authentic characters in pursuit of empathetic goals in the face of significant obstacles.

8. *Humor:* You can usually make us cry more fully when you have first made us laugh. Meaningful drama is always supported by a range of human emotions.

9. *Theme is subsidiary and integral to the dramatic action:* We know what a story is and we know what an advertisement is. If you promise a story, make good on your promise.

SOME ADDITIONAL NOTES ON NARRATIVE WRITING

Narrative drama is some of the most difficult playwriting. But it is such an important technique for turning a true story into drama. My comments here come out of my own struggles to work within this form.

My plays tend to limit narrative devices to a single character. For additional examples, see my plays *When Scott Comes Home*, *September Bears* and *Kin*. Jeffrey Sweet uses narrative writing in his play *Bluff*, and fascinatingly, he lets all the characters make narrative comments. This device of Sweet's is similar to the narrator/character of *Story Theatre* by Paul Sills. In *Story Theatre* the narrator/character is present in each person, but we do not meet the actor except hidden within the character. In Sweet's convention, the actor is able to appear and comment upon the character that he or she is playing. In other words, both the actor and the character are always present on stage. Sweet's version is narrator/character/actor—all three.

The guidelines below are useful when a character is narrating his or her own true story. For example: "This is Jerry White's story. I play Jerry White. I'm walking down the street near my house. . . ." But it is also possible for these devices to be applied to a narrator who is telling someone else's story. (Parenthetical examples are from *Bluff* by Jeffrey Sweet.)

1. Narrative lines are almost always present tense.

2. Narrators may talk about something they are doing or something someone else is doing.

3. Narrative lines should mostly describe actions. The verbs should be specific and evocative. ("I barrel down the stairs, yelling. . . ."; "She smiles, and in one smooth motion, removes . . .")

4. Narrators may sometimes evoke the environment, efficiently filling in scene, sound and light. ("Stan Getz is playing on the CD. Candles are throwing our shadows onto the walls.")

5. Narrative lines should be brief and even incomplete. Incomplete sentences sometimes keep the audience engaged by letting them complete the

sentence themselves. ("But if he's going to be okay—")

6. State facts when necessary, but actions advance plot.

7. Quick comments to the audience are appropriate. ("GENE: Dental supplies paid for your ballet lessons. EMILY: [to audience] I'm biting my tongue.") Even out of character. ("And that's it for this character. I'll be back later, playing someone else. Hold your breath.") And note that narrators can have attitude!

8. Words compress large actions/movements, jumps in time. ("I have to wear dark glasses for maybe a week, and I will end up with a little scar.")

9. Words sometimes replace and thus evoke large emotions. ("LORING: A scream." In this example, LORING is the character who has screamed. Instead of actually screaming, he has used the word "scream" for the simple reason that we are compressing action and emotion into a short time at this point in the play. To use an actual scream would seem funny and out of place unless you have a longer set up to provide the appropriate context for the scream.)

10. Actors move seamlessly between speaking narration to audience and speaking in dialogue to scene partners. (NEAL: [to audience] I sublet my apartment to the niece of a friend. EMILY: [referring to

audience] Do you think they care? [to Neal] You
can have that closet.)

11. Physical properties are seldom necessary, and thus
when they are used, they take on great significance.

12. Actors can stand aside and watch, listen, and even
comment as actors.

13. Narration to explain time or place can sometimes
happen best even after the dialogue of a scene has
already begun. ("GENE: Sadists and goofs. EMILY:
I don't know. NEAL: [to audience] It's October
now.")

14. Narration is especially valuable when you have
non-human characters. For example, an actor
playing God could say to the audience, as they
walk in, "I play God. And no, I don't really know
how God walks."

Enacted Prayer

This prayer form is very simple, but our teams have learned a few techniques. Perhaps it will be helpful for me to share them here.

Format of Enacted Prayer

1. A prayer leader asks for a request or praise.

2. The leader identifies specific roles in the prayer and actors immediately volunteer by moving onto the stage. The roles include actors to represent God at work. If enough actors are available, three actors are assigned to represent God at work. Other roles are known people, but sometimes we have represented illness, weather, unborn children, etc.

3. After casting the prayer, the leader repeats who each actor represents. The leader also summarizes the request or praise in a sentence.

4. The leader begins the prayer by addressing God and affirming that we have come to offer a real prayer (without summarizing this time).

5. Music begins under the leader's introduction to

the prayer. Actors also begin.

6. The prayer is enacted silently.

7. No props are used, but chairs or stools are helpful.

8. When the action has arrived at the desired praise or request, the actors freeze in mid-action. They should try to freeze at the same time, but it is not a requirement. If an actor is not finished, they may continue until the story is complete, even if other actors have already frozen.

9. After several seconds, the leader completes the prayer by affirming that this prayer is prayed in the name of Jesus. No further summary is necessary. Music out.

10. If it is a small group, the leader may ask the person who gave the request if what they saw enacted was indeed what they wanted us to pray. They may also comment on how the prayer affected them if they wish. An adjustment to the prayer is permissible and sometimes necessary. As verbal prayers sometimes are prayed via a process of struggle for words, so enacted prayers sometimes are prayed through a process of struggle for images.

Further Suggestions

1. There should always be a sense of journey or story in the prayer. This usually means stepping into the

past so we see the set up to the situation.

2. God's movements can be abstract. We are affirming in these prayers that we do not know everything God is doing and we believe God is at work in ways we do not always understand.

3. Characters do not look at God, but actors representing deceased persons or unborn persons may see God. It can be a wonderful affirmation to see someone we have lost to this life coming into the presence of the Lord.

4. Actors representing God should try not to leave anyone alone if at all possible.

5. Actors representing God wear sashes to help everyone remember who they are.

6. God characters can help the action by providing telephones for phone calls (and then helping the actors know when the phone call is over and they can hang up—cued with a simple touch). The actors representing God are the only ones who have the freedom to look around and see every location at once, so their guidance in the prayer is greatly appreciated.

7. Focus is important with so much going on. Try to be aware of when you are and are not the main focus, and help the audience know where to look. When your part of the story is finished, move to the side or turn away so you will not distract from the other action.

8. The prayer leader usually needs a microphone to share the request with the entire congregation and speak over the music.

9. Make sure you know exactly what is being prayed for, and encourage specificity. One helpful question to ask is something like, "How will you know when this prayer has been answered?" or "What would it look like if that happened?"

10. Music: use music without words, ideally stuff that no one will immediately recognize. The idea is to focus on the images, and the music should help facilitate that. It often works well to choose music that does not correspond precisely to the assumed mood of the prayer. Contrast can be rich. Choose music that has some build and development to it. Live music can also work very well because it can respond to the action. Our team has used voices, piano, and drums.

Exercises

1. Practice freezing together while miming separate activities.

2. Rehearse God helping or caring for people doing simple tasks. Explore different ways that those representing God might move.

The Value

The central value of enacted prayer is that it provides a specific and memorable image of an unseen reality.

The Fisherman and His Wife

(story from the Grimm brother's collection)
adapted for the stage by Jeff Barker, as inspired by Paul Sills

Fisherman
Alice
Fish

(May be played by three actors, but this script is prepared for two actors.)

AT RISE: Two chairs upstage.

JEFF
(speaking rhythmically at first)
Once there was a fisherman.

KAREN
Who lived with his wife.

JEFF
In a pretty little hut.

                    KAREN
It's a ditch.

                    JEFF
It's a hut.

                    KAREN
It's a ditch!

                    JEFF
In a hut in a ditch by the sea.
        (JEFF blows her a kiss.)
And he'd blow her a kiss.

                    KAREN
        (KAREN waves him away with disgust.)
And she'd wave him goodbye.

                    JEFF
And off to go fishin' was he.
And one day as he sat there fishin'
Just about driftin' to sleep,
Up from the brine
Came a tug on his line,
Sharp, and strong and deep.

        (JEFF screams. He grabs the mimed pole with both
        hands.
            KAREN has become the fish. Perhaps she does this
        with an adjustment of her shawl. The two characters see
        one another but using offstage focus.)

JEFF (continued)
(as she comes into focus, he freezes)
What in the world?

KAREN
I am an enchanted fish.
Do not take me home for supper.
Throw me back as fast as you can.

JEFF
That's no problem. I don't want nothin' to do with a talking fish.

(JEFF tosses the fishing pole.)

JEFF (continued)
The fisherman was so excited that he threw his entire pole into the water.

KAREN
And the fish darted straight to the bottom, leaving a long streak of blood behind.

JEFF
The fisherman went home to his hut in the ditch. Hello, love, I'm home.

KAREN
What'd you catch?

JEFF
Well, I didn't catch nothin'.

KAREN

Why do I even ask.

JEFF

Actually I did catch one fish, but he said he was enchanted, so
I threw him back.

KAREN

You caught an enchanted fish?

JEFF

Yeah. Just one.

KAREN

Did you ask him for something?

JEFF

Ask him for what?

KAREN

Anything. Three wishes.

JEFF

Three wishes?

KAREN

Yes. Did you ask him for three wishes!

JEFF

No.

> KAREN

Two?

> JEFF

No.

> KAREN

One?

> JEFF

No.

> KAREN

You're an idiot.

> JEFF

Oh, boy.

> KAREN

It's not too late. Go back to the fish.

> JEFF

He swam away.

> KAREN

Call him back. Tell him you want a wish.

> JEFF

I don't want a wish.

> KAREN

Yes, you do.

JEFF

Well, I wish I didn't.

KAREN

Tell him, tell him—tell him you're tired of living in a ditch—
you want to live in a cottage. Tell him he owes you and you wish
for a cottage. Get goin'.

JEFF

We haven't even had supper yet.

KAREN

Go get us a cottage first. We can have supper later. Now go.

JEFF

The fisherman's one wish in the world was to make his wife
happy, and so he went. On the way, he made up a little poem.
He said to himself, "Enchanted fish must like poetry." When he
got to the water's edge, he called out,

Roses are red
And the ocean is blue
Fish, how I wish
To be talkin' to you.
A woman was given me
From God above
Some know her as Alice
But I call her love.

KAREN

And the fish returned. Hello, fisherman.

JEFF

Hi. How'd you like the poem?

KAREN

It was cute. What do you want?

JEFF

Oh. My wife says that since I was the one what caught you and let you go that I should have asked you for a wish.

KAREN

What does your wife want?

JEFF

Well, she wishes to live in a cottage because she doesn't care for the—

KAREN

Go home, fisherman. Your wife's wish is already granted.

JEFF

Saying that, the fish swam away. And the fisherman immediately went home. When he got home, his wife was standing in the doorway of a cottage.

KAREN

Now do you see the difference between that ditch and a real house?

JEFF

Oh boy!

KAREN

Come in here. Look. There's a kitchen. With cupboards. That's real linoleum. Wipe your shoes. Living room. Laundry room. Bedroom. Look out back.

JEFF

Is that our garden?

KAREN

Go pick some tomatoes. I'll make stew.

JEFF

We sure will be happy here.

KAREN

Well, maybe.

JEFF

And so they had supper.

(They put the chairs facing one another and bow their heads in prayer.)

JEFF (continued)

Giver of all gifts. We are grateful to thee. Amen. And after supper, they went to bed.

(They put the chairs together and go to sleep. The wife tosses and turns in her sleep.)

KAREN

Fisherman. Wake up. The floor plan of this cottage is not right.

Go back to the fish and tell him we need to make a change.

JEFF
The floor plan?

KAREN
Yeah. We need a bigger bedroom.

JEFF
Well, love, why go to the fish? I can build a thing or two.

KAREN
Yeah, right. Look—just go to the fish and tell him we want a big stone castle.

JEFF
A castle?

KAREN
Yes. With one of those ditch things around it—a moat.

JEFF
No. I'm not going back to the fish. We're just going to make him mad.

KAREN
If he can make a cottage, he can make a castle. It's no big deal.

JEFF
Can we at least have breakfast first?

KAREN

Castle first, breakfast later. Now go.

JEFF

To tell you the truth, the fisherman did not want to go. But the fisherman's one wish in the world was to make his wife happy, and so he went. On the way, he tried to hum a little, but it was difficult to keep his mind on it. When he got to the seaside, the sky was overcast, and the water was gloomy. The fisherman stood where he had first met the fish, and he called out,

Roses are red
And the ocean is gray.
Fish, how I wish
We could talk here today.
A woman was given me
From God above
Some know her as Alice
But I call her love.

KAREN

And the fish returned. Hello, fisherman.

JEFF

Hi, fish.

KAREN

How'd you like the cottage?

JEFF

The cottage was really cute. We had tomato stew last night.

KAREN

Well, you're quite welcome.

(The fish turns away.)

JEFF

No, wait fish, don't go yet. My wife says the floor plan ain't right.

KAREN

The floor plan?

JEFF

That's the same thing I said.

KAREN

What does she want?

JEFF

Well, she said since it was so easy for you to make a cottage, that you could make a big stone castle just as well, but I told her that I could build a thing or two—

KAREN

Go home, fisherman. Your wife's wish is already granted.

(KAREN starts to leave.)

JEFF

Um, fish, I almost forgot, she also wants one of those ditch things—

KAREN

It has a moat. Goodbye fisherman.

JEFF

Saying that, the fish swam away. And the fisherman immediately
went home. When he got home, his wife was standing at the
entrance to a big stone castle.

KAREN

See what I told you.

JEFF

(amazed)

Whoa. Is this really ours?

KAREN

Your problem is that you set your sights too low.

JEFF

Are we allowed inside?

KAREN

We live here, you idiot.

JEFF

They went inside and there were golden tables and chairs. And
servants and cooks. And a sculpture garden and a forest and a
stable and a kennel.

KAREN

Those are real Persian rugs. Wipe your feet.

JEFF
We sure will be happy here.

KAREN
Well, maybe.

(They move the chairs apart, as if at the ends of a long table.)

JEFF
And so they sat down to dinner.

(They put the chairs facing one another and bow their heads.)

JEFF (continued)
Giver of all gifts. We are grateful to thee. Amen. And after dinner, the servants brought supper. Giver of all gifts. We are grateful to thee. Amen. And after supper, they went to bed.

(They turn the chairs front, but far apart, and climb into bed.)

JEFF (continued)
Goodnight, love.

KAREN
Goodnight.

(JEFF closes his eyes.)

                    KAREN (continued)
The next morning, the wife awoke with an idea. Fisherman.
Wake up.

                    JEFF
Good morning, love.

                    KAREN
I have an idea. Go to the fish and tell him you want to be the
king.

                    JEFF
This was such a silly idea that the fisherman thought he was
dreaming.

          (He giggles in his sleep.)

                    KAREN
Hey!

                    JEFF
I'm not dreaming am I?

                    KAREN
No. Now go to the fish and tell him you want to be the king.

                    JEFF
That would be a lie. I don't want to be the king.

                    KAREN
You don't want to be the king?

JEFF

No.

KAREN

Okay, fine. That's fine. That's just fine. You go to the fish and you tell him that I want to be the king.

JEFF

The wife left quickly before the fisherman could get dressed, and when he went looking for her, he could not find her because there were so many rooms in the castle. Now the fisherman's one wish in the world was to make his wife happy, and so he went back to the sea. On the way, he said to himself, "This is such a silly idea, but the least I can do is to say I tried." When he got to the seaside, the sky was green, like the calm before a storm. The fisherman stood on the shore and called out,

Roses are red
And the ocean is dark.
Fish, how you'll laugh
When you hear of this lark.
A woman was given me
From God above
Some know her as Alice
But I call her love.

KAREN

And the fish returned. I didn't expect to see you so soon, fisherman.

JEFF

Well, I'm sorry to bother you, but I think you're going to laugh when you hear this.

KAREN
What does she want now?

JEFF
You're not going to believe it.

KAREN
You'd be surprised what I'd believe.

JEFF
Well, just brace yourself. My wife sent me over here to tell you that she wants to be the king. Isn't that a good one?

KAREN
Go home, fisherman. And greet the new king.

JEFF
What? What? What? But the fish was gone. And the sky was green. So the fisherman went home.

(He places two chairs next to one another.)

JEFF (continued)
When he got home, he discovered that his wife had become the king.

(He sits.)

JEFF (continued)
And he had to wait all day for an appointment. When he finally

got in to see the king, he said, Love, what's it like to be the king?

KAREN

No one calls me love. You'll have to stop that.

(She snaps her fingers and indicates that he should kneel.)

JEFF
(kneeling)
You surely must be happy now.

KAREN

That just goes to show you how little the common people know. I no longer want to be the king. Go back to the fish. Tell him I want to be the Pope.

JEFF

You what?

KAREN

The king does not repeat an order.

JEFF

Love.

KAREN

Watch it.

JEFF

But king, we're not even Catholic.

KAREN

We soon will be.

JEFF

There is only one Pope in all the world.

KAREN

Precisely. Guards. Escort him out.

JEFF

The fisherman did not want to go. But the king's guards had long faces and longer spears. So the fisherman went that very night. The sky had turned from green to black. It was raining hard.

Roses are red
And the ocean is wet.
Fish, how I wish
That we never had met!
A woman was given me
From God above
Some know her as Alice
But I call her love.

Fish!

KAREN

I'm right here fisherman.

JEFF

Fish. My king has ordered me to tell you that she wishes—that she wishes—oh, boy.

KAREN

Fisherman.

JEFF

Ohhhh, what.

KAREN

Go home. Your king is now the Pope.

JEFF

Fish! Fish!! But the fish did not answer, and it was so dark, the fisherman could not see a thing. So he went home. And when he was a long ways off, he heard chanting. And when he came a little closer, he saw rows of men in red, red robes. But that was as close as he could get. So he lay down at the foot of a sycamore tree. And fell asleep.

KAREN

In the morning, the Pope arose for her morning prayers, and she watched the sun break in the eastern sky. And she began to cry. And she said to her attendant, go find the fisherman.

JEFF

And they found him sleeping outdoors, and they kicked him awake and drug him into the presence of the Pope with profound apologies.

KAREN

Fisherman.

JEFF

Yes, lo—, um your majesty—, your high—, your holiness.

KAREN

Fisherman. I saw the sunrise this morning. Did you see the sunrise this morning?

JEFF

No. I was asleep.

KAREN

Well it was beautiful. And I said to myself, "Why can I not make a beautiful sunrise?" Go, fisherman. Go to the fish. Tell him that I would be the maker of the sunrise.

JEFF

And the fisherman got to his feet. And he spoke in a quiet calm voice. Alice. The fish cannot make you the maker of the sunrise. Not you or anyone else.

KAREN

I've told you before, and this is the last time I will say it: the least we can do is try. And with that, the Pope gave a little flick of her wrist, and the guards all dressed in silver grabbed the fisherman and carried him off to the sea.

JEFF

When they came to the shore, the sun was gone. The lightning cracked, and the thunder roared. The wind screamed and the rain stung like knives. The guards drew their swords, and the fisherman cried out,

Blood is red
And the ocean is black.
Fish, how I wish

I could take it all back!
A woman was given me
From God above
Some know her as Alice
But I call her love.

KAREN

And the fish rose to the surface of the water.

JEFF

Fish!

KAREN

Yes, fisherman.

JEFF

My wife wants to be—

KAREN

Yes, fisherman.

JEFF

My wife—

KAREN

Yes.

JEFF

Wants to be the maker—

KAREN

Of the sunrise.

JEFF

Yes.

KAREN

No, fisherman. There is only one maker of the sunrise. Go home fisherman. Go home.

JEFF

And the fisherman opened his eyes. And all was quiet. And the enchanted fish and the guards in silver were gone. And the fisherman immediately went home. When he got home, his wife was standing all alone.

KAREN

Hello fisherman.

JEFF

Hello, love.

(She blows him a kiss, which he catches with true joy.)

JEFF (continued)

Once there was a fisherman.

KAREN

Who lived with his wife.

JEFF

In a dirty old ditch.

KAREN

It's a hut.

JEFF

It's a ditch.

KAREN

It's a hut!

JEFF

In a hut in a ditch by the sea.
And he lived in that hut
with Alice his love.

KAREN

As happy as happy can be.

END OF PLAY

Bibliography

Bierma, Nathan. *Bringing Heaven Down to Earth: Connecting this Life to the Next*. Phillipsburg: P&R Publishing Company, 2005.

Boogaart, Thomas A. "Drama and the Sacred: Recovering the Dramatic Tradition in Christian Worship." In *Touching the Altar: The Old Testament for Christian Worship*. Edited by Carol M. Bechtel. Grand Rapids: Wm. B. Eerdmans, 2008.

Borgman, Paul. *Genesis: The Story We Haven't Heard*. Downers Grove: Intervarsity Press, 2001.

Brown, Tim. *Perspectives*. Grand Rapids: Reformed Church Press, May, 2002.

Buechner, Frederick. *Wishful Thinking: A Theological ABC*. New York: Harper & Row, 1973.

Calvin, John. In Charles Garside Jr., *The Origins of Calvin's Theology of Music: 1536-1543, Transactions of the American Philosophical Society*. Vol. 69, part 4. Philadelphia: The American Philosophical Society, 1979.

Craddock, Fred B. *Craddock Stories*. Edited by Mike Graves and Richard F. Ward. St. Louis: Chalice Press, 2001.

Goldberg, Natalie. *Writing Down the Bones: Freeing the Writer Within*. Boston: Shambhala, 1986.

Holmes, Arthur. *The Idea of a Christian College*. Grand Rapids: Wm. B. Eerdmans, 1975.

Jenness, Morgan. In *Dramaturgy in American Theatre* edited by Susan S. Jonas and Geoffrey S. Proehl, 409–411. New York: Harcourt Brace & Company, 1997.

Lewis, C. S. *Letters to Malcom: Chiefly on Prayer*. Orlando: Mariner Books, 2002.

Luther, Martin. *Martin Luther's Basic Theological Writings*. 2nd ed. Minneapolis: Augsburg Fortress, 2005.

Lutheran World Federation. *Nairobi Statement on Worship and Culture* (1996). http://www.worship.ca/docs/lwf_ns.html

Miller, Donald. *Searching for God Knows What*. Nashville: Thomas Nelson, 2004.

Liturgy and Confessions. New York: Reformed Church Press, 1990.

Long, Thomas. *Testimony: Talking Ourselves into Being Christians*. San Francisco: Jossey-Bass, 2004.

Morgenthaler, Sally. *Worship Evangelism*. Grand Rapids: Zondervan, 1999.

Norris, Kathleen. *Amazing Grace*. New York: Riverhead Books, 1999.

O'Connor, Flannery. *Mystery and Manners*. New York: Farrar, Straus, and Giroux, 1969.

Pullman, Philip. Quoted in Laura Miller "Far From Narnia." New Yorker Magazine. New York: Condé Nast Digital, December 26, 2005. http://www.newyorker.com/ archive/2005/ 12/26/051226fa_fact

Ruth, Lester. "A Rose By Any Other Name: Attempts at Classifying North American Protestant Worship." In *The Conviction of Things Not Seen: Currents in Protestant Christianity in the Twenty-First Century*, 33-51. Grand Rapids: Brazos Press, 2002.

Sacrosanctum Concilium. Rome: Vatican. December 4, 1963. http:// www.vatican.va/archive/hist_councils/ii_vatican_council/ documents/vat-ii_const_19631204sacrosanctum-concilium_en.html

Sares, Mike. "Scum of the Church: How the drive for 'excellence' is driving young adults from the church." *Out of Ur* blog. August 21, 2006). http://www.outofur.com/archives/2006/ 08/scum_of_the_chu.html

Sills, Paul. *Paul Sills' Story Theatre: Four Shows*. New York: Applause Books, 2000.

Sweet, Jeffrey. *The Value of Names and Other Plays*. Evanston: Northwestern University Press, 2008.

Vandevort, Eleanor. *A Leopard Tamed*. New York: Harper & Row, 1968.

Webber, Robert. *The Divine Embrace*. Grand Rapids: Baker Books, 2006.

White, James. *Documents of Christian Worship*. Louisville: Westminster John Knox Press, 1992.

Witvliet, John. *Worship Seeking Understanding*. Grand Rapids: Baker Book House, 2003.

Wren, Brian. "God Talk and Congregational Song: An Interview with Brian Wren." *The Christian Century*. May 2, 2000, 507.

Index